# THE POWELLS
# OF NIGERIA

## 87 YEARS OF MISSIONARY SERVICE

### by David Gasperson

2

## Foreword

From the very beginning of the research and writing of this book I knew it would be a major project. Discovery of so much primary source material increased its difficulty.

The first draft looked like a jigsaw puzzle of quotes. I worried the flow of the story would be lost. At the same time I felt a responsibility for setting forth the words of the people themselves, knowing full well those letters and obscure books and pamphlets would be inaccessible to most readers. It was my wife, Teresa, who was the first to read the manuscript and who encouraged me to leave the quotes intact. My thanks to her for that encouragement.

The next concern was how to cite the sources in a way usable to the reader. At first I had the references in parentheses at the end of each quote. Enter two very good proofreaders both of whom wanted that method changed. One wanted footnotes, the other abbreviated notations within the text referring to the bibliography. I settled on footnotes.

I offer my great thanks to these two proofreaders who brought trained outside eyes to this manuscript. Scott Peterson is Associate Director for Global Research at The

4

International Mission Board of The Southern Baptist Convention, Richmond. Sherry Matthews is editor and publisher of *The Sampson Independent*, Clinton, North Carolina.

Correspondence and even manuscripts often carry the unique character and style of the writers. Especially in the case of J. C. Powell's, I was constantly confronted with the choice of smoothing his English or preserving what is often his uniqueness and power. At various times I did both. Despite all efforts, my own errors may still have leaked through into print. Other times I have acted with intentionality to preserve uniqueness and even errors as part of the richness, geography and/or era of the primary source.

My thanks to the people of Warsaw Baptist Church. When they became aware of Teresa and my venturing into "things Powell," they supported us fully. They see the work, apparently, as Teresa and I most certainly do, as the extension both of my ministry and of the ministry of the church. Many know Mary Hester and remember Carlyle and Rosa Powell and are happy they are being acknowledged for their years of dedicated service.

Readers will find at the end of the book a timeline and an annotated bibliography, an awareness of which is useful from the start.

Following the professional recommendations of the readers, the many citations from letters are footnoted simply noting from whom, to whom and the date. I've kept the contractions and informal style which in recent years has become my own - perhaps to the consternation of Sherry and Scott.

Who'd have thought that, at sixty-six years of age, I would encounter a family whose ministry flourished more than half-a-century before my own and that learning and writing about them would turn out to be life-enriching if not life-changing for me. May the reading be so for you.

David Gasperson
Warsaw
July 24, 2018

## Introduction

I don't believe in chance, happenstance, coincidence, luck. When I find an unexpected juncture on life's journey, I try to be especially alert to what God may be doing in bringing that set of circumstances together.

I was blessed to come to serve Warsaw Baptist Church in North Carolina in 2013. Once there, I was pleased to discover the church fellowship hall named after career missionaries who had served collectively for 87 years in Nigeria. I was pleased as well to find a Powell history room with mementos of their lives and work.

Standing before the dedication wall in Powell Hall with the oil pictures of Carlyle, Rosa and daughter Mary Hester, I have always felt humbled. Though I myself am entering the senior years of a life-long ministry, it's been carried out in the comfort of American churches. There is something humbling about standing under the pictorial gaze of those who ventured into the undeveloped regions of Africa a hundred years ago and helped lead countless people to Christ and firmly establish Baptist work in Nigeria.

I had the opportunity to meet with Mary Hester Powell several times in the course of my early years at Warsaw. Mary Hester lives in a retirement community in Greenville, N. C., having never been married nor had any siblings. Her small apartment displays a number of Nigerian items, made by the nationals and each with a special meaning to her. Her mind is sharp though a stroke hindered her and forced many months of recovery and therapy.

By 2017 I'd served Warsaw Baptist Church and lived in Warsaw long enough to become very familiar with both. I was also looking for a new project. I dabble in construction and even have my contractor's license. When the town manager said he wished I'd look at a particular huge but rundown house on Pine Street, I was intrigued. Often as I'd driven along that main street I'd looked at the house and had remarked to my wife how it had such potential. But it sat abandoned and decaying for the whole time I'd been in town and folks reported its dilapidated state actually went back much further.

Nevertheless, the house was pictured and described in a book of the historical homes in Warsaw.[1] I learned it was the J. A. Powell house. Hmm... Powell. But then, there are a lot

---

[1] W. Frank Ainsley. *The Historic Architecture of Warsaw, North Carolina.* Garden Club of Warsaw, 1983. 62.

of Powells around Duplin and Sampson counties.

Fairly quickly I learned Julius Alexander Power was father of Carlyle Powell, the missionary. He'd been a farmer and store owner who came to Warsaw in mid-life to build a house in 1909. I guessed he'd hoped his almost-grown family of 12 children would use the house as a place to which they could return as they needed and for reunions. J. A. Powell had been right. Members of the family kept coming back to that 14-room home on Pine Street for decades.

Annie Kate, the youngest of the Powell children, had been a victim of childhood polio. Confined to a wheelchair, she nevertheless lived out a long life in the family home and had a career in the business office of the town's furniture store. She was the one who kept the family together, planned reunions and the like. She was the family member who managed her brother Carlyle's affairs back in Warsaw while he and Rosa were abroad. A sharp business mind, she had built, helped build and rented several houses in Warsaw and two large vacation homes at Carolina Beach the family used for getaways.

Kathleen (also Carlyle's younger sister) came back after her divorce. She had a master's degree in Home Economics and taught for years. The remainder of her time was absorbed in genealogy and family history. She left behind many filing cabinets of research, multiple huge albums of collected information, self-published books and innumerable envelopes of clippings, cards, photographs and letters.

Members of the family who lived in the house later on had amassed great quantities of ... stuff. Then there was no one living locally. The house was closed up. But it didn't remain closed. Vagrants forced entry, came and went at will, tossed all the stacks and files, ate there, slept there... and more.

As best I could tell, no one of the J. A. Powell lineage remained in the immediate area. The owner of the house was out-of-state. We got her name and address from tax records and I wrote her. Would she be interested in selling the house?

We bought the house with remaining contents included in October 2017. The town began to find out about that purchase and shook their collective heads at what the Baptist preacher and his wife had undertaken.

My wife and I began to wade in with trash bags and snow shovel. Dozens of trips to the landfill followed. But it wasn't that simple. Mixed in with the trash was the life and history of a huge Down East family and the missionary son they had produced.

Soon I realized this was not just a filthy old house. This was a trove. A huge amount of information was available on every member of the family, their offspring to three generations and the allied families with which they'd married. The preacher of the family figured prominently. Not only were there clippings, photos and anecdotes of the family, but mementos and even furniture pieces including some from Nigeria.

An internet check found no biography of Carlyle and Rosa Powell. A quick email to the International Mission Board of the Southern Baptist Convention revealed a great interest in making their archives available as much as privacy laws would permit.

I looked up from a four-inch-thick album of Powell genealogy. Me ... this church ... this house ... these resources... Mary Hester's availability....

I don't believe in coincidences.

What is it that causes a boy... a girl ... otherwise ordinary, to early on have a deep relationship with God? What shapes the calling in a young person's life with such bold relief no amount of difficulty in carrying it out can stop them? What causes a couple to spend a life-time and their daughter many years in an inhospitable climate during desperate economic and war circumstances for little salary and almost no recognition? Those are some of the questions that need answers. They are relevant in the twenty-first century as they were in every preceding era. They are good reasons for a brief account of these lives.

But there is another reason for me to write in addition to the "coincidences" of my encounter with the Powells. Almost nothing has been written about the Powells and their service. A huge history of Christianity in Nigeria, the 804-page *A Heritage of Faith* published in 2017 by Ayodeji Abodunde carried not a mention of the Powells and only a few paragraphs on Southern Baptist work at all.

The few Southern Baptist resources published on Nigeria are no more helpful. George W. Sadler was a missionary colleague of the Powells and a friend. But when he wrote *A Century in Nigeria* there was only a single paragraph about the family:

"Some missionaries, however, devote the major portion of their time to general station work. Rev. and Mrs. J. C. Powel [sic] have spent many years in this process: Building churches, supervising native workers, teaching teachers, helping in woman's work, and performing many other tasks. It must be a source of great satisfaction to them to have their only daughter, Mary Hester Powell, who was born in Africa, join them in the service to which they have given the best years of their lives" (139).

Perhaps it is the general work of "station missionary" that made them easy to pass over. Their efforts were spent in the daily grind of living among the indigenous people, helping them, doing hard work of construction, teaching, administration, organization and discipling as well as countless little tasks and through it all talking about Jesus Christ and the salvation he accomplished for all.

More needs to be said about the Powells, and about countless other self-sacrificing missionaries. It is important not for the elevation of human accomplishment. They would never seek or even tolerate such an effort. It is important because noticing lives which are so totally dedicated to carrying out their callings exalts their Lord Jesus Christ. Here I seek to carry forward the trajectory of a family of faith and service. I seek to demonstrate the results of divine calling that directed young lives on a path that would persist lifelong and even beyond one generation.

J.A. Powell family ca 1890
baby in center, bottom looking away
is Carlyle

## Chapter 1
## The Red-headed Thinker

*I shoveled out the trash at the house with a snow shovel. I dug through piles of magazines, old bills, cards, ... rats nests. There it was, amongst stacks of random genealogical notes. I almost tossed it - 18 single-spaced, typed, legal-sized pages, written no doubt for his younger, genealogist sister, Kathleen - "Some Tid Bits by J. C. Powell". These were stories of his youth. I would find even his own daughter did not know they existed, although I would also later find some of the stories recounted in letters to Mary Hester in 1939.*

The original Powell "plantation" - every good sized farm was a "plantation - was in Sampson County where "Alec" (as Julius Alexander Powell was nick-named) had been born son of Confederate Colonel Luke Powell.

In his early years, J. A. Powell must have been a rough young man. Carlyle recounted of his father: "Be it said to his credit he never drank more than one quart of whisky in one day unless it happened to be on special occasions...." As the kids came on he settled down and by midlife was known often as Deacon Powell. When he married Mary Emma Bourden, they took up a farm from her family not far from Warsaw, just inside Duplin County.

Julius Carlyle Powell was born January 22, 1890 at the old McGowan-Bourden-Powell plantation near Warsaw. Twelve children were born to Julius Alexander and Mary Emma Powell. "My father had the habit of telling people that the chimney fell down and killed all but twelve."[2] Seven were boys. J. C. talked about them as his mother's football team. He called himself their quarterback and said he was the "red-headed thinker" of the bunch.

Carlyle, himself, and his sister Kathleen recorded some of his memorable moments as a precocious little boy:

"Our family had to have big hog killings to provide meat for the family and the tenants who lived on the place. This was long before the day of commercial balloons, and at hog killing time, it was a race to see who could claim the place nearest the post. That one got the bladder from the first hog that was dressed. The bladder was blown up on a reed and used as a balloon. Soon after a hog killing, when Carlyle was a tiny boy, they came out crying and announced that Grandma Bourden had died. Carlyle immediately said, 'I speak for that bladder.'"[3]

---

[2] J. C. Powell to Mary Hester Powell, August 29, 1939.
[3] Kathleen Powell Snyder, *What Will They Do Next*, 91. Hereinafter "Snyder".

"Jim Moore, a cousin ... lived in Wilmington, but always spent Christmas at the Powell home. Every year, he came with five gallons of oysters for the family and an especial gift for his Aunt Mayme - a small bottle of brandy and two camphor gums to make the next year's supply of camphor. The boys and their father ... each had filled large, old fashioned soup bowls with oysters which they seasoned with salt, pepper, and vinegar. On one occasion, the vinegar gave out before it got to Carlyle, and he went to the pantry to replenish it. Mistaking the brandy for vinegar, he generously poured it on the oysters. The next thing anyone knew, he dashed out on the side porch and threw the oysters, antique soup bowl and silver fork into the garden. Coming back into the dining room, he admonished the whole crowd, 'Don't eat those oysters, they are rotten.' ... That was Carlyle's first and last taste of alcoholic spirits. In fact, Rosa says he told her if she ever gave him a drop of it for any reason, he would leave her."[4]

He remembered his younger sister being stricken with Infantile Paralysis (Polio). For six months she could not move anything other than her head. He remembered being required to sweep the bare-dirt yards. He

---

[4] Snyder, 91-92.

remembered birch switches the kids would have to cut for their own punishment.

He remembered the swimming hole and equaled it to a bath: "When a boy learns to dive he learns the art of getting a decent head washing. He may not actually get his head as clean as he thinks he does but he gets a mental cleaning and that is the cream of a bath anyway. Oh! THE FUN HE HAS COUNTS."[5]

The other kids apparently called Carlyle "Mamma's Little Angel," from time to time, deriding his generally good behavior and the preference they believed their mother showed for him. But "Mamma's Little Angel" was certainly capable of mischief.

"There are a few times in a boy's life when he really feels big.... When his ma makes him a real shirt and he has suspenders and not buttons to a waist to hold up his pants. When dad puts him between the plow handles and allows him to plow by himself. When he can pull one over on dad and mother both and use some tobacco and they not find out. He really has an exalted opinion of himself when these happen." Tom, one of the farm hands had told him: "'Go to the house and get me a plug of 'bacca and charge it to me.' My father would buy it by the box and let the hands have it a

---

[5] "Tid Bits".

plug at the time, so as not to have to bring them each a plug every time he went to town." Carlyle asked Tom if he could try some. Pretty soon he began to "feel sick and sorta blind." Then he fell unconscious for about two and one-half hours. A few months later on a dare he slipped his mother's snuff box and took a dip. He didn't know how to use snuff and he swallowed some. Soon the fireplace began to "move and look like two places so I spit at whichever one I took to be the right one."[6] He declared he never wanted anything more to do with tobacco. But in a letter to Mary Hester he admitted when he was a pre-teen he and cousin Marvin were tasked one summer with curing the tobacco. They smoked nearly a whole Sears-Roebuck catalog that year, using it to roll their cigarettes.[7]

There was the time he was made cart driver when the boys were shoveling out the barn, hauling compost and drilling it into the fields. He was too little to do either shoveling or drilling, so he was put on the wagon seat and made mule skinner. Molly the mule was gentle and easy going, but slow. When she didn't get started, he gouged her with a pitchfork. Brother Luke took him to his Ma and she "switched ends" of the switch on him.

---

[6] "Tid Bits".

[7] J. C. Powell to Mary Hester Powell, September 29, 1939.

When he was whipped by his teacher at school for foolish behavior, he got it again from Ma at home that night. That time she used a black gum switch, saying: "I will teach you how to go to school and disgrace me with your smart-eleck conduct." He said of that whipping it was the "first and only time I ever got down on the floor and wallowed for a whipping."[8]

In a fight with brother Halstead, he took off his shoe and chased him into the house. In his parents' bedroom, J. C. saw a figure raise up on the bed and thought it to be his brother. "I took advantage of the opportunity and let the old brogan drive. ... The sole caught Dad right on the nose and the heel struck him right in the forehead. ... Dad just walked in the other room and pulled down his razor strap. ... When Dad turned me lose that night I knew the difference in a mother or sister trying to teach me the path of honor and the wrath of a father trying to reform a devil bent son that had no more self control than to hit his Daddy before he looked to see who he was. It looked to me like my pants would explode, they were so hot."[9]

Brother Davis stole some apples from him: "We had a right decent fight and ended

---

[8] "Tid Bits".
[9] "Tid Bits".

by his threatening to cut my head if I said another word and put the point of his knife on my head to prove his intentions. When he removed the knife I grabbed up a stick and hit him in the mouth. His mouth began to bleed and I began to beg him not to tell ma. My pleading was all in vain. The blood of my brother cried against me with convincing evidence before my mother."[10]

As a boy he would listen to the dogs chasing rabbits. He'd learned the sound they made when they were about to catch their prey and he would run to the dogs, take the rabbit away from them and bring it to his mother to cook. She never knew where the kill had come from.[11]

---

[10] "Tid Bits".
[11] J. C. Powell to Mary Hester Powell, September 1939.

Carlyle Powell as a young man

## Chapter 2
## The Preacher in the Family

*Stacks and stacks... piles and piles. A head-tall, metal cabinet on the enclosed back porch crammed with four-inch-thick notebooks of plastic covered family history notes.*

Jeanie Powell in the tenth grade in Florence, South Carolina produced a 4-page essay "A Remarkable Family" in which she summarized the life of each of her aunts and uncles in one paragraph: "Carlyle, the fifth son, is the preacher in the family and has spent most of his adult life as a missionary in Nigeria, West Africa. He has been credited with building more churches in Africa than any other one missionary. In his youth he was a great athlete and had a great love for big game hunting. He is a good man, unselfish not only with his earthly possessions but with his very life."

But how does a farm boy become a missionary?

Certainly the answer lies partly in family life where the Bible is read regularly and family prayer observed. That was so with the J. A. Powell family.

Church is important. The family in those early days was at Johnson Baptist Church in the little community of Lanefield, some three miles southeast of Warsaw. In completing forms for his foreign mission service, Carlyle indicated conversion on a Wednesday night in 1904 - he would have been 14. The same service record lists 1908 as the year of his calling to Christian ministry. Again at a Wednesday night prayer meeting, Carlyle announced to the Johnson Baptist Church he had been called to preach. He first preached there as well.

It was in the tiny Lanefield School that Carlyle got his early education. He enrolled in 1895. His sister, Cary, was teaching there at the time. He would later describe the rigor of that education as "one hour studying and six hours playing." Those were days when local schools were largely one or two room affairs. Public education was only gradually taking hold. Many Baptist academies were sprinkled across the landscape which offered high school and preparation for college. Many also provided dormitories for students who came from some distance for their education.

Warsaw had such an institute, established by good Baptists early in the 1800s. Warsaw Baptist Church had been launched by Eastern Baptist Association in 1855 largely to serve the spiritual needs of the students and teachers of the institute. Today the Warsaw Church building stands where the old institute once stood.

But when it came time for Carlyle's high school education, the family did not choose Warsaw. Instead, he was enrolled at the Dell School.

Dell School opened in 1902 in a community eventually called Delway - south of Clinton toward Wilmington. It emerged as a boarding school with multiple buildings and was part of the Baptist system of secondary schools from 1909 until 1922. It closed in 1923. Five remaining buildings are a historical site.

In the years Carlyle attended, Dell would have been a new facility. Not yet Baptist by official connection, it still had strong spiritual underpinnings. Since J. A. Powell had come from the Clinton area, he may well have known some of the principle people involved in Dell's start-up.

"When Dell School opened for the session, Carlyle Powell was the first student. He helped to get the campus ready for the other students. Often he would walk home for the weekend, a distance of 16 miles. When time came to go back, his Father would offer to let one of the boys take him back - at least part of the way - but he always refused, saying, 'Oh no, I can walk it.' His mother would prepare him a lunch which he would invariably eat before he got to Aunt Nan's house - a half mile away - so he would not be bothered with carrying a package."[12]

Let Carlyle tell the tale from the last page of "Tid Bits":

"It was a great day for the Powell home when the young preacher started out in search of his education. The word education was a new term to him, in the past he had only known it as 'book learning.'

"His entire family had done their best to get him ready for the ordeal. His brother Davis told him frankly he was a fool, then explained by saying 'You aught to have gone off and acted several years as a traveling salesman before you declared you were going to preach, if you are going to preach to people you aught to know how people think. ... This being about his first introduction to the term education, he wondered how much it would cost him. Davis added 'My bank account and yours will be one until you have finished school.' This sounded mighty good for he was sure it would take at least two years to finish, one year in high

---

[12] Snyder, 91.

school and one in college. He did not have but $17.00 and he did not think that would be sufficient to take him through.

"When he started away some suggested that he take the big trunk that grandpa left to the family. But the smaller one was decided upon.... But he had three full changes of clothes besides a Sunday suit one of the boys had given him. He also had an extra pair of Sunday shoes that had not been half-soled but once and a dandy good pair of black socks to match them.

"When he reached the high school he was about the most versatile person on the hill. He knew three languages - profanity, slang and farm expressions. Besides this he was loaded with two types of theology: simple honesty and crowd harangue....

"The poor boy was leaving home for his first time in life, and he broke down and cried like a whipped child when he got out of sight of the house. When he reached the school, ... he was determined to conquer his heart aches with over physical exertion. When a wagon load of students would arrive, he would rush out and jump the yard fence and help get the trunks to their places. ...

"Here are a few of the first lessons he learned. Fools don't always stay at home, some go off to school. Money takes wings and flys from you when you get away from home. Learning is not measured and sold in stipulated quantities to be poured in your head, but by hard work and cramming it gets there. What you get and do not remember is worthless to you in the future. Stomach and heart aches both have their causes; and can be avoided if we will but only keep our minds open and our mouths shut.

"When he met the faculty, he and the faculty both laughed for they each knew there was rough sailing ahead for the other."

Although J. C. Powell would complete college and seminary, he never lost his colloquial voice. Nor did his spelling and grammar get far from the furrow of the field. Rosa's English in her letters is very proper and polite, in neat handwriting. Carlyle's handwriting was so bad hardly anyone (including me) could read it. Colleagues demanded he type his correspondence. Then the worn-out ribbons of the typewriters and his lack of keyboard prowess still made them difficult. Half the time he misspelled Charles Maddry's last name, though he reported to Maddry. His writing is colloquial and often carried expressions and vernacular.

At Dell school everyone had the chance to talk about their faith on Sunday nights (Perhaps a Baptist Young Persons' Union). He had to write out his talk to get through the experience.

Carlyle was made Secretary of the Eastern Baptist Association BYPU. At the Association's meeting, he had opportunity to give a five-minute talk. "I made my talk on tithing and made a statement in my speech that no man could give God anything until he had first paid his tithe." One of the ministers present "took offense at my statement and got up and shook his finger in my face and said, 'I give you to understand young man I can make God a gift whether I ever pay the tithe or not. The tithe is no longer binding on me, sir. I am under a higher law of Grace. I do not consider myself tied down to any Old Testament law.' The longer this brother talked to me the hotter and the redder in the face he got. I have never quite understood why he should take the advantage of a young man's first public speech but he jumped on me with both feet and hands and tried to make a monkey out of me that day."[13]

The choice of subject for such a pivotal early speech demonstrates an early and firm

---

[13] J. C. Powell to Mary Hester Powell, date unclear.

commitment to tithing as an absolute requirement. Rosa and later Mary Hester would always give meticulous attention to the tithe as well. On a regular basis, letters home would ask whoever handled their domestic finances to be sure their tithe was paid. When any extra remuneration or gift was received, no matter how small, they tithed.

The BYPU for Eastern Association was divided into "fields" with each youth speaker assigned one. Carlyle was assigned a church whose pastor also answered his speech at the end. It's hard to imagine the trauma the young preacher must have felt at twice being challenged. It in no way curbed his fervor.

All the while he was at Dell school, Carlyle kept up his participation in church. At Evergreen Baptist Church in Delway he was ordained to ministry in 1910.

Dell School graduating class 1912
Rosa and Carlyle top center

## Chapter 3
## "The Fur Of Her Nerves
## Rubbed the Wrong Way"

*There was a newspaper clipping from decades past recounting the story of J. D. Hocutt and his family. There was a copy of a chapter from a book on missionary romances. I quickly tracked down a used copy of the book.*

Jefferson Davis Hocutt (1861-1932) was born in Rocky Point, North Carolina not far north of Wilmington. His family was poor and he was the youngest, leaving him with a sense he needed to stay around home and work the farm. As a result, he was only educated through the fifth grade.

Hocutt married in December 1890 and it was through his wife, Hester Katherine Murray, that the couple came to have a small farm in Pender County, a few more miles north of Wilmington. There at the little crossroads of Ashton they settled to farm and raise a family of 14 children, the 15th having died as a baby. The house he built there still exists. The farm, less than 55 acres, was saved from a developer in 1975 and is now a summer day camp introducing 700 young campers a year, many out of Wilmington, to the joys of rural life - somehow very appropriate to the Hocutt heritage.

Though not well educated, J. D. Hocutt was a supporter of education even helping keep up the little one-room school house he allowed on his farm property. After all, his big family was one of the largest suppliers of students.

J. D. also loved the Lord and he loved preachers. He would travel miles to hear a preacher who seemed to be especially gifted. And even though he knew he could never be educated as many ministers were, he was ordained as a Baptist preacher and served small churches round-and-about the Wilmington Association wherever he found the opportunity. Hocutt would often leave on a Saturday night on a white horse to go to his appointed place to preach.

It was a small farm. There was never much money. To make ends meet, Hocutt rented additional land and staggered crops to have some income producing crop coming in just about all the time. He started a sausage business, selling personally on the streets of Wilmington.

One of their sons who grew up to be a preacher and an Associational Missionary in Buncombe Baptist Association (Asheville, North Carolina) wrote a little book on the family. It became the primary source for information when the *Warsaw-Faison News* ran a multi-page feature on the Hocutt clan. The family estimated the couple spent $28,000 educating their family - a fabulous amount for the early 20th century. Ten of the kids in all went to college. Most became teachers. The newspaper reporter having added up their teaching experience bannered the Hocutt family had taught for 195 years.

Rev. Hocutt made a name for himself in Pender County for honesty and for commitment. When the open range issue was being legislated in Raleigh to determine whether herds had to be fenced or could range openly, Hocutt ran for and was elected to the legislature and served in 1919. (He was pro-fence.) When that one issue was settled, he refused to run for reelection and returned to the farm.

Such was the family into which Rosa Beatrice Hocutt was born on September 27, 1891. As the first born of the Hocutt brood, Rosa apparently early on developed the seriousness so often evidenced in the eldest who is called upon to help raise the younger children.

Like the little school on the Hocutt property, the church they attended met in a

small wooden structure with only one room.
Riverside Baptist Church sat on the Northeast
branch of the Cape Fear River six miles
southeast of Burgaw. The church in later years
merged with Burgaw Baptist Church, but in
Rosa's childhood the Hocutts and one other
large family made up most of the attendance.
Her conversion came at that church when she
was 14.

"On March 5, 1944, it was voted that we
accept the proposal of nearby Riverside Baptist
Church that it consolidate with our church. 73
members were received in a body from the
church on March 26, 1944. Riverside was the
home community and church of Mr. and Mrs.
J. D. Hocutt, Sr., who reared and educated a
large family of 14 children, including 2
ministers and a missionary, in a noble manner
of Christian courage and cooperation of the
highest order."[14]

It is a hard thing for a large family when
the eldest child must go away to school. Hard,
as well, for that eldest daughter to tear herself
away from responsibilities at home. But Rosa
Hocutt knew she would be needed to help pay
the way through school for those younger
brothers and sisters. She wanted to teach. That

---

[14] Howard Holly. *Brief History of Burgaw Baptist Church: 1884-1974.*

meant a better education. And so at 16 Rosa traveled north ... to the Dell school.

"Carlyle's love for Rosa was 'love at first sight.' For Rosa, it came slower. Carlyle had been at Dell a couple of weeks helping with the construction of a building.... Finally the big day came and the college sent a team of mules and a wagon to the Railroad Station in Rose Hill to pick up the young ladies.... Carlyle was on the front porch of the dormitory when the wagon came in sight. He spotted Rosa on the wagon and declared, 'That is the girl I am going to marry.' With that, he leaped off the porch, pole vaulted over the fence, then opened the gate.... Dignified Rosa was insulted at the actions of one so spontaneous. She remarked, 'I do not know who that uncouth boy is, but I do hope I do not have any classes with him. It would be most distasteful to have to be around him.'"[15]

Carlyle must have cut a fine figure of a young man judging from pictures of the era. A later passport showed him five feet eleven inches tall with blue eyes.

The attitudes of the two toward each other could not have been more polar opposite. He was rambunctious and demonstrative, she reserved and serious. Carlyle was smitten from

---

[15] Snyder, 92.

the start. Rosa wanted nothing to do with him. "Later he described her that day as 'a dignified confirmed old maid of sixteen with the fur of her nerves rubbed the wrong way.'"[16]

Rosa ignored Carlyle all through school. Even when he came to preach at Riverside Church, she seemed unimpressed. Both ended up dating others, but Carlyle continued to seek her favor. When they were about to go off to different colleges, he finally convinced her to write him ... but only as a friend.

---

[16] Ina Smith Lambdin. *Then Came Spring: And Other Missionary Love Stories*. Self-published, 1969, 1. Hereinafter "Lambdin."

"Sky" Powell the athlete

## Chapter 4
## "Sky"

*In the "Powell Room" at Warsaw Baptist Church is a hollowed-out half gourd with a twine "chin strap". It'd been presented to Carlyle Powell as a going away gift when he and Rosa retired and left Nigeria. Painted yellow, the "helmet" had lettered on the front "Sky."*

Finding a way through high school and on into college was not easy going for farm kids of the day. Carlyle was 22 and Rosa 21 when they headed off to college, he to Wake Forest and she to Meredith. Those two schools were the leading Baptist colleges in North Carolina. They were also close to one another - in Wake Forest and Raleigh - the same Wake County. That was long before Wake Forest made the move to a new campus in Winston-Salem.

The relative proximity of the two schools apparently enabled Carlyle to make trips to see Rosa. It was common in that day for boys from Wake to travel by train to see the girls at Meredith. The *Howler* of Wake Forest College was published every spring by the literary society and served as the college's annual. In the 1913 "Follies of the Foolish" section appeared this account: "'Sky' Powell, having been left at Neuse on his way to

Raleigh to attend a concert at Meredith, and being forced to walk in, arrived rather late. Miss Meredith, observing him black with coal dust, with one shoe on his foot, the other one under his arm, exclaimed, 'Where have you been for the last four hours?' ... Powell: 'I has been a-coming.'"

The entry succeeded in poking fun at Powell's farm expressions and also highlighted what must have been many trips he made to see "Miss Meredith" - certainly Rosa.

Apparently his frequent trips by train to Raleigh to see Rosa became renowned. The 1913 *Howler* "History of the Ministerial Class" section remarked jokingly: "We deeply deplore the fact that some of our members have erred by the way. Harris and Powell have won for themselves the name of 'hobo' by riding and attempting to ride trains without tickets."

It was at Wake Forest that Carlyle became interested in football. Despite the fact he had never even seen a football game played, he was among several Freshmen to try out as walk-ons for the team.

Carlyle's football buddies gave him the nickname "Sky." I asked his daughter, Mary Hester, why he got that nickname and she said every ministerial student was dubbed "Sky." She said that was because they pointed people's attention heavenward. Later I found a note saying the football team called all ministerial students "sky pilots."

"Sky" was a nickname that stayed with him for life, although only used occasionally. His brothers and sisters called him Carlyle, most colleagues called him J. C. To Rosa, he was Carl. But once in a while through his whole life, he would sign a letter home or be addressed by family and friends as "Sky."

If the name "Sky" stayed with him, so did football. In the final months of his life, the invalid "Sky" Powell was loaded into the back of a van by his church buddies and taken to watch a high school football game. It was the thing he most wanted to do.

Half the varsity football squad at Wake Forest were freshmen in the 1912 season. They were not a winning team, but the coach reported in the *Howler*: "Although we won only two games, when we take into consideration the fact that the team was far ahead of any that has represented the college since the game was reestablished here we must term the season a success." Clearly Wake Forest was not known as a football powerhouse in those days.

"When a Freshman at Wake Forest, he wanted to go out for football. He talked things over with a Professor who said, 'If you can keep your temper, go ahead.' He played in the first game he ever saw. During one of the games, his opponent wanting to get him mad and thus disqualified and put out of the game, called him an 'S.O.B.' His answer, 'Oh, well, we can't all be well born,' and continued to play, not only for four years of undergraduate work, but also as a graduate student after he had been in Africa for a while."[17]

"Sky" Powell turned out to be very athletic. He lettered in football and track in 1913 and 1914, played intramural baseball and was captain of the track team his senior year. The 1916 *Howler* yearbook said of him, "'Sky' is perhaps the best all-round athlete on the hill, and in debate he is as good as they make them. ... 'Hard as nails' against things which he considers wrong, in all other respects he is kindly, genial and sympathetic." His stats showed him six feet tall and 185 pounds. As "Sky" Powell's health declined in his senior years, one of his college friends, Attorney Lee Carlton, wrote him "I remember you as one of the best football players I ever saw. You were the strongest man - per pound - I ever saw."[18]

---

[17] Snyder, 91.
[18] Attorney Lee Carlton to J. C. Powell, January 19, 1966.

At Meredith, Rosa was in the college choir, house president and played basketball in 1916 and 1917. Her senior annual, *Oak Leaves*, described her as "an unpresuming girl who yet aspires to become a minister's wife, and she is mighty close to her goal, too." If that was the case, "Sky" Powell had no clue.

A sense of calling to foreign missions emerged in the hearts of both Carlyle and Rosa separately but both early on. For Rosa a drawing to missions had arisen as early as high school days. When he traced his own sense of calling, "Sky" Powell wrote in his service record he had begun feeling the compulsion in 1912. It would take some time for the calling to become definite and they did not seem to be on the same track early on. One time Rosa would want missions and Carlyle would not. Then it would be reversed.

Education proceeded apace. Carlyle graduated with an overall grade average of 89. But the two were making very different preparations. Carlyle knew early on he would go on to seminary. Rosa always intended to teach. For Rosa, the future seemed more structured and demanding because of the all-to-real awareness her help was needed at home with the remaining Hocutt children and her financial support needed for their education.

Carlyle graduated from Wake Forest in 1916, Rosa from Meredith in 1917. Both degrees still hang on the wall in the Powell Room at Warsaw Baptist Church.

At the end of her college days, Carlyle was in South Carolina working. He wrote her a lengthy letter telling her he wanted them to be more than friends. He was verbose by his own account "I had a regular tropical rainy season of words and a Sahara Desert of thought."[19] His flowery words did him no good. A week later the answer arrived - she wanted friendship and that was all.

Rosa would teach first at Dell School, then at James Sprunt Institute in Kenansville, North Carolina when an outbreak of flu closed Dell. Carlyle went to Louisville.

---

[19] J. C. Powell to Mary Hester Powell, November 18, 1939.

**J.A. Powell House, Warsaw NC**
**July 1919 wedding reception**
**Carlyle and Rosa are two on far left**

## Chapter 5
## 12-Word Courtship

*A picture kept showing up in the stacks of records in the Powell House. There'd been lots of copies made. It showed a gathering of some 60 people on the front steps of the Powell House and was labeled "July 25, 1919". This was one of the earliest reunions at the Powell House ... and Rosa and Carlyle's wedding reception.*

Louisville, Kentucky must have seemed a world away from Eastern North Carolina. The flagship seminary for the denomination, The Southern Baptist Theological Seminary brought a national and international exposure to students otherwise poorly traveled and poorly exposed to the larger world. Scholars, denominational leaders and missionaries came and went from the classrooms and hallways.

But the broadening of Carlyle's horizons never dulled his heart. Like Rosa, his sense of calling to foreign service ebbed and flowed, sometimes reaching a fever pitch, sometimes being tempered by family and financial realities.

"Sky's connection with Eastern North Carolina was maintained with summers and vacations back in Duplin County and the surrounding areas. About the time he entered

Southern he served brief pastoral roles in the only American churches he ever served - at Snow Hill and Fremont.

Carlyle's love for Rosa never waned. If anything, the distance increased its fervor. "Carlyle always insisted that his and Rosa's courtship consisted of exactly 12 words. He was at the Southern Baptist Theological Seminary, and she was teaching, helping to put her younger sisters through school. He wrote a 16-page letter to her, and on the middle of the eighth page, set off in a paragraph by itself were the words, 'MY LOVE I GIVE, YOURS I SEEK.' Three weeks passed and still no answer from Rosa. Elliott Stewart, his seminary roommate, said he thought he would go crazy waiting for her answer. She would write, but she did not refer to his proposal. Finally it came. On the eighth page of a 16-page letter in a paragraph to itself were these words: 'MY LOVE I GIVE UNRESERVEDLY.' That was it: 12 words."[20]

Those simple lines of commitment each to the other "Sky" Powell considered to have been the extent of their courtship. "That was the only sweetening we ever put in the coffee."[21]

---

[20] Snyder, 92.
[21] J. C. Powell to Mary Hester Powell, November 18, 1939.

From that moment on their love for each other was never in doubt. Just how they would bring together their two individual senses of calling and their responsibilities for their families remained to be resolved.

"Since her high school days Rosa had been thinking of foreign mission service. Sometime after she had pledged her love to Mr. Powell, she wrote him that she had an impression that perhaps she should give her life to foreign missions. He wrote back that he had no such idea for himself but that he would not stand in her way...."[22]

Later, when she went to his college anniversary celebration to meet him, she told him she'd decided to stay home. He was relieved. "Sky" Powell proceeded to ask her father for her hand in marriage.

Carlyle had almost finished his seminary training and the calling to missions was still not resolved in his heart. Then John Anderson, a close friend, died in an accident in China. Ina Smith Lambdin believed it was a seminal event that brought a focus to his call to missions.

---

[22] Lambdin, 5.

But this time, Rosa resisted. Apparently she continued to feel responsibility as the eldest child in her family.

Powell wrote her "If God leads the way, come and go with me to Africa. If not, you are free." Then he prayed "Lord, if you want her to go with me, let her wire me her answer within ten days...." On the tenth day two letters arrived from Rosa. In the first she wrote: "I do not want to go unless I feel that the Lord is calling me personally. I do not want to be a hindrance to his cause. You had better count me out." In the second letter she wrote "I am praying over it." Conflicted, Carlyle lay down and took a nap. He was awakened by the Western Union courier with a wire: "Have decided to go to Africa with you. Am volunteering to the Foreign Mission Board as your wife to be." He dropped back onto his pillow and cried for joy and relief.[23]

"When they went before the Foreign Mission Board for their interview before being appointed as missionaries, Carlyle had waxed oratorical in expressing his feelings in the matter, his call to service in the foreign field, etc. When he had finished, they called on [Rosa]. All she said was, 'May I go with him.'"[24]

---

[23] Ibid.
[24] Snyder, 92.

Toward the end of his missionary career, "Sky" wrote in his own hand for his Foreign Mission Board Service Record an account of his calling to mission service:

"My call was of long standing.

My surrender was on my knees in a Louisville park.

The day I surrendered, I volunteered.

I left it in God's hands and volunteered for Africa - Nowhere else.

I was appointed within three months after my surrender.

I believed in June 1919 I was called of God, knew it in March 1946 and I still believe I was called to Africa."

On July 24, 1919 Carlyle and Rosa exchanged vows before her minister father at little Riverside Baptist Church in Ashton, North Carolina. Kathleen Powell was one of the bridesmaids. Everyone knew the new couple was destined for mission service in Africa. It was written into J. D. Hocutt's wedding ceremony. One of the newspaper clippings on the event read in part: "As the bridal party was leaving the church, the procession was preceded by little Miss Betsy Hocutt, a sister of the bride, dressed as an angel and carrying a map of Africa." Rosa's brother, himself to become a Baptist preacher and denominational leader, later wrote, "The decorations for the ceremony were so arranged that the aisle in which they entered was named America and the aisle they marched out was named Africa. The words were spelled with flowers fastened to the wire ... for the curtains that divided the Sunday School classes."[25]

The next day the reception was held in Warsaw at the Powell house on North Pine Street. It became the occasion of the annual family reunion. Sixty people gathered on the front porch for the photograph which still exists today.

---

[25] H. M. Hocutt, *Struggling Upward*, 47.

**Oyo Baptist Chapel**

## Chapter 6
## Africa Only

*Mary Hester Powell sat in her wheelchair outside a wire storage bin in the basement of her life-care facility in Greenville. With her was Kathryn Hamrick, a Hocutt cousin. My wife and I poured through boxes and suitcases of clothes, books, papers, slides and photographs. I was being given full borrowing privileges. Among the things I took back to church for a children's session on the Powells and missions was a wooden plaque in the shape of Africa with Nigeria outlined in a different-colored wood.*

There was never any doubt in the minds of Carlyle and Rosa Powell as to where God had called them to serve. It was and remained throughout their lives only Africa. Writing about his calling near the end of his career, Carlyle said, "... I volunteered ... for Africa – nowhere else."

The Niger, at 2600 miles the third longest river in Africa, was always a center of trade and population growth. Modern Nigeria is the largest nation on the continent with a population which approaches the 200 million mark. Its economy surpassed South Africa in 2014 to also become the largest on the continent.

The Niger and its tributary, the Benue, divide the country into three parts. Seasons can best be described as "rainy" (April - November) and "dry."

It's important to understand the dynamics of religious development in Nigeria. Not only is it a pivotal nation on the developing continent of Africa, but today is also one of the flash points with Islamic fundamentalism.

Islam had penetrated the region as early as the eleventh century, Catholic monks in the fifteenth. The region was, during the tenure of the Powells - and remains today - Muslim in the north and Christian in the South. But indigenous religion with some 400 or more deities continued long to be a major influence on daily life. Social customs including polygamy remained resistant to either of the major religions.

Nigeria particularly and Africa generally are some of the fastest developing regions for Christians. As Christian demographics continue to shift from Western nations to developing nations, Africa is pivotal. Some estimates have it that by 2050, seventy percent of Christians will live in Africa, Asia and Latin America.

It was only in conjunction with the slave trade that European attention was brought to the Niger delta region. Exploiting the constant friction between African tribes, local tribes and their European backers enslaved millions, transporting them all over the world, largely to the New World in slave ships and under inhumane conditions.

Slavery shaped the mentality of the population in Western Africa while it was going on and since its eradication. Constant strife between the tribes combined with suspicion and sometimes violence against incoming white residents led to a growing exertion of British power. The principle coastal town of Lagos was invaded by the British in 1851 and annexed in 1861. The entire region became a British protectorate in 1901.

Of the three major people groups in Nigeria, the Yoruba on the west bank of the Niger were the dominant. They had also lost a lot of their people to the slave trade. Especially after the British Parliament outlawed slavery in 1807, freed slaves were returned to Sierra Leone. Many had become Christians. Soon they realized from whence they had come. Some of them returned to Yorubaland – a few as Christian missionaries.

Protestant denominations had begun to send missionaries to Western Africa by about 1800. Almost immediately after the formation of the Southern Baptist Convention, the Foreign Mission Board was sending missionaries, beginning with Thomas Jefferson Bowen in 1850.

T. J. Bowen set a high standard for mission work, producing a scholarly book on Central Africa in 1857 and later a grammar and dictionary of the Yoruba language which was published by the Smithsonian Institution. Baker James Cauthen would write of him, "Southern Baptists have not, even yet, brought to reality the comprehensive program for the evangelization of Africa which was outlined in Bowen's book and which captivated his soul."[26]

Southern Baptist work got its start at the towns of Lagos, Abeokuta and Ogbomoso. Civil war was an on-again-off-again reality for the region despite the presence of the British. By 1860 only two SBC missionaries were left in Lagos. The Civil War in the United States roughly coincided with a civil war in Nigeria. Combined, they brought a virtual end to mission work begun in Nigeria at such a high cost.

---

[26] *Advance: A History of Southern Baptist Foreign Missions.* Broadman, 1970, 140.

Southern Baptist mission efforts in Nigeria got a restart in 1874 when William Joshua David was appointed and William W. Colley, a Black minister from Virginia, set apart as his helper. They found Christians at Lagos and were successful in forming a church there in 1876. Soon thereafter churches were organized at Ogbomoso and Abeokuta.

Moses Stone was a talented Nigerian who soon emerged to lead the First Baptist Church in Lagos. In 1888 he broke with David and withdrew his membership from First Church. Nearly 200 members joined him, leaving a bare 24 to carry on the work at First. The group with Stone as their pastor formed Ebenezer Baptist Church. "This schism which originated in Lagos was felt throughout the country and placed a strain upon relations between missionaries and African leaders."[27] That was really the beginning of the Native African movement in the churches.

In 1894, Stone returned as pastor of FBC, Lagos and began efforts at reconciling the two groups. Mojola Agbebi became pastor of Ebenezer. This "Spurgeon of Nigeria," as he was called, ranged far and wide preaching evangelistically and starting churches. In 1914 he was elected the first president of the Yoruba Baptist Association. A unity of the factions was

---

[27] Ibid., 145.

achieved which would eventually produce the Nigerian Baptist Convention. By 1900, half a century after Southern Baptist efforts began in Nigeria, the denomination could report only 6 churches, 6 outstations and 385 members.[28]

Eventually Southern Baptists enjoyed enormous success in their mission work in Nigeria. Churches, schools, mission houses, hospitals and denominational structures proliferated. In large part, that success was because of the Powells and other missionary families like them who dedicated many years or entire lives to the spread of the news of Jesus Christ to people who did not know that Gospel.

Several new missionaries arrived in Nigeria at the beginning of the twentieth century. Dr. George Green and his wife Lydia came in 1907 when he began service as the first medical missionary for Nigeria. Ewart Gladstone and Addie Louise Biggs MacLean came the next year. They were Canadian, but appointed by the Foreign Mission Board. Dr. Basil Lee and Mrs. Josie Still Lockett arrived in 1910. He practiced medicine, preached and served as missionary advisor first at Abeokuta, then at Oyo.

---

[28] Ibid., 146.

Between 1919 and 1924, spurred on by the hope of additional income from the Seventy-five Million Campaign, a total of 22 new missionaries were appointed for Nigeria. Among them were J. C. and Rosa Powell.

Thousands of Christians and hundreds of churches and schools owe their spiritual origins to the work of Southern Baptist missionaries. But the work of these missionaries is omitted in the story of Christianity in Nigeria as told by some historians. A very recent history of Christianity in Nigeria claims to be exhaustive (and is exhausting). Its 804 pages gives whole chapters to relatively minor sects. But the work of Southern Baptists is given only a handful of paragraphs in the whole book and the Powells are not mentioned at all. The downplaying of Southern Baptist efforts in such an extensive coverage may be due to the Pentecostal or political leanings of the author. If nothing else, that virtual omission underscores the need to highlight the work of the Powells and others missionaries like them who played so great a role in Christian Nigeria.

The civil wars and tribal conflicts of the nineteenth century which had placed so many missionaries in peril had largely been quelled when Britain made Nigeria a protectorate in 1901. British law held sway in the courts.

British soldiers and British-trained and supported police were in the streets. Victorian morality began to make inroads into a culture which, some believed, still practiced human sacrifice and most assuredly practiced polygamy.

Among Nigerians there was an appreciation of British stability in their region. There was also a distrust of Western culture as the root of the slavery which had so decimated the region for three centuries.

Throughout all the British period there was an uneasy tension between British and Nigerian culture which was true in any colonial environment. It would build in intensity and fuel the independence movement by the middle of the twentieth century.

Human sacrifice was illegal by British law and solidly rejected by missionaries from all denominations and sects. But it was still occasionally practiced in the shadows. Simply called "murder" by the authorities, Nigerians and the missionaries knew indigenous religious beliefs were sometimes the root cause.

"...we have a ruler of the city who is in favor of human sacrifice. ... There was a sacrifice here about three weeks ago. The government will put it down as murder and we do not put out the word that it is human sacrifice, but we all know what it is. When the woman was found her throat was cut out and one foot cut off. We have had five people mysteriously missing just like this in about two years."[29]

Carlyle would go on to say in the letter that parents panicked if their children were missing for even a moment. It's necessary, perhaps, to mention such atrocities to draw attention to the spiritual darkness of the region in those days of mission work.

Many of the African beliefs came into direct conflict with Christian teaching. For example, it was commonly thought that the dead live again in a child. "Babatunde" was a common name for a child and meant "the father has again returned." It was given when the boy was born shortly after the father's death and meant they thought the father returned in the child.[30]

Of even greater prevalence was the practice of polygamy. Again, British law would

---

[29] Carlyle Powell to Charles E. Maddry, Foreign Mission Board Executive Secretary, November 2, 1935 from Shaki, Nigeria.
[30] Carlyle Powell described it in a letter to Mary Hester Powell, December 19, 1939.

not recognize more than one wife. Practitioners would simply maintain two homes in different villages or on different streets. The authorities would either never know or look the other way.

Even when it came to the churches, there was the tendency not to confront polygamists, particularly since it was sometimes prominent and wealthy men who maintained more than one wife. Some native Christian leaders and even some missionaries insisted polygamy was cultural. While almost all Christians would assert monogamy, many said a man who had more than one wife should not be excluded from membership in the churches or from baptism and maybe not even from leadership.

When J. C. and Rosa Powell arrived on the field in 1920 the polygamy issue was in hot discussion. Carlyle's letters back to the Foreign Mission Board for many months would decry native pastors and even the occasional missionary who were tolerating polygamy. Powell never did. For him, biblical mandate on the matter of marriage surpassed any cultural consideration. When he was in a position to make a change, he would not leave a polygamist in leadership.

**Girls dormitories under construction
Abeokuta, Nigeria**

## Chapter 7
## Master Builder, Gifted Teacher

*This time I was wading through several boxes of photographs, slides, manuscripts and correspondence loaned to me by Mary Hester Powell herself. I found there four pages in Rosa's own hand describing their first voyage to Nigeria.*

Carlyle and Rosa's original intention was to sail for Africa right after the wedding. As would often happen, they were delayed and did not leave until January 6, 1920. Even then they were forced to lay over two weeks in England. That turned out to be a very nice but belated honeymoon.

### The Trip Over

"The first trip over, Rosa said, 'they should not have charged him but half fare for he walked at least half the way.' (Pacing up and down on deck, that is.)"[31]

Rosa Powell, herself, gave an account of their passage: "On Jan. 6, 1920 Rev. and Mrs. W. H. Carson[32] and Rev. and Mrs. J. C. Powell set sail from New York for Nigeria, West Africa. The voyage to England was slow and cold and the seasick experiences on the part of

---

[31] Snyder, 93.
[32] William Henry and Grace Schimmel Carson.

the women were most trying. After about two weeks we arrived in Liverpool and were told to wait for Rev. and Mrs. Pinnock,[33] Miss Susan Anderson and Miss Cora Caudle." They traveled about, toured London, shopped, saw Cambridge and Oxford. "In the meantime Mr. Carson pricked a finger on the pin attached to a price tag. This became infected and, in spite of treatment, became so painful that we had to leave him in a town on the way to Liverpool." They sailed without the Carsons and on the way to Africa learned his infection had become gangrenous and resulted in the loss of part of his arm. The Carsons ended up staying in England several months for his recovery. "The two weeks trip down the West Africa coast was anything but pleasant for Mrs. Powell. When the ship arrived in Lagos on February 28, Dr. B. L. Lockett met the party and said immediately to himself that Mrs. Powell was already a patient for him."

"Our first stop was Freetown, Sierra Leone. We anchored several hundred yards from shore. The natives came out in small canoes to take the passengers and luggage ashore. The skill with which these boatmen handled their canoes fascinated us. They scrambled for the loads which were being lowered by the derrick, but they always gave way to the first man who touched an item.

---

[33] Samuel George and Madora Carstin Pinnock

"Boys were diving for pennies thrown to them from the deck of the ship. They would spring from their canoes and catch the pennies before they reached the bottom of the harbor. They were excellent swimmers and, like all boys, preferred the barest of swimwear. Most of them wore only a loin cloth. Indeed, one boy had only a silk beaver hat someone had given him."[34]

## The Language

The Powells lived in Oyo and Shaki, Nigeria through many of the years in Africa. Carlyle valiantly studied the Yoruba language under a well educated native tutor. The language did not come easily.

"Mrs. Powell and I are tugging after this bable of a language and it comes slow, but work on and keep hard at it must be our only motto."[35]

Even two years later, Carlyle was still struggling to fully master the language. "I note with a great deal of satisfaction that you are

[34] J. C. Powell and David Gasperson, *Impressions of Nigeria*, 9. Hereinafter "Powell, *Impressions*".
[35] J. C. Powell to J. Franklin Love, Foreign Mission Board Executive Secretary , March 19, 1920.

going to be able to buckle down to language study seriously again, and hope you will put your time in well on that phase of your work, because it would be most unfortunate for you if you do not in this first service period get a very good hold of the Yoruba tongue. You will be able to get it better now than you ever will again, so I am hoping that with some of the heavy duties that have been on you now being taken off, you will find it possible to do a great deal of work on the language study."[36]

Carlyle did master the language, eventually translating the New Testament book of Acts into the indigenous language and writing short books which appeared in both English and Yoruba.

## Building

The practical matter of building churches and schools consumed the overwhelming majority of Carlyle's time in the pre-war service periods. A fast start for the Powells' mission work was required due to the departure of one of the key missionaries who had been responsible for construction. From the beginning of Christian mission work in Nigeria, the work was characterized by the

---

[36] T. Bronson Ray, Executive Secretary of the Foreign Mission Board to J. C. Powell, October 13, 1922.

early construction of three buildings at each station and thereafter in any village that would support the work: a mission house, a church and a school. Especially in the early years of the twentieth century there was much need for construction as the work expanded.

Dr. Lockett had been the missionary in charge of construction. Almost as soon as the Powells arrived, Lockett returned to the States. Carlyle immediately took over those construction projects.

"I wish you could have seen these natives eyes stretch when they saw me pick up a truss that would weigh at least a ton if not 2500 pounds and handle it as easy as if it had been a baby. One of them I set on the wall in ten minutes. But you see my task was to teach them how to use leaver power. I was a new man and they had no faith in my plans at first but after they saw one of those big old trusses set safely in the wall, after that I have had no trouble with their confidence in my plans. ... If I had not had some practical experience during my high school career in house moving I would have been right up against it."[37] Mary Hester Powell on one occasion prepared notes to introduce her Dad and said of his building,

---

[37] J. C. Powell to T. Bronson Ray, Executive Secretary of the Foreign Mission Board, June 8, 1921.

"Daddy is said to have 'introduced the plumb line' into Nigeria."

"In the part of Africa where they lived, there were few large trees suitable for building, yet Carlyle was dubbed by the Foreign Mission Board as 'Master Builder,' after having been responsible for building more than 50 churches."[38]

The family record of Carlyle's service in building churches often emphasized his construction, referring often to him as the "Builder" or "Master Builder." It's a designation that may have been enhanced by their love for him. However, a colleague added strength to that legend.

Alfred Conn Donath, who served in Nigeria for many years with the Powells before returning to serve as pastor to churches in the U. S., wrote for Carlyle's service record: "Powell was called 'The Builder' by the missionaries and nationals. He knew construction work, and knew how to encourage and enlist the Nigerians in building their church buildings and schools. He could get more done for the money than anyone on the field. If he did not have half a dozen building projects under way all the while, his fellow workers would jibe him for 'loafing.'"

---

[38] Snyder, 93.

To Rosa, it seemed Carlyle was away all the time. Even the nationals commented he was gone a lot during this period of their work.

"Sometimes he and some of the natives would walk 30 or 40 miles, cut down trees which they would carry on their shoulders to the saw mill, and later carry the lumber on their shoulders to the building site."[39]

Building in remote areas was demanding. "I am right now putting the roof on a church out 13 miles from here where I go out and work and sleep in the old school. I have spent two weeks already there and I think it will take me two more."[40]

Earliest churches were built of mud and gravel walls because materials were readily available and the native builders knew how to use them. "Foundations were dug to the clay and gravel laterite level about 18-24 inches below the surface. Then clay and top soil were mixed together with water to form a paste. That paste was rolled into balls about the size of a double fist. That size was easy to throw to a builder on the wall who would throw it into the wall and press it down by hand. Courses of 15 - 24 inches thick and up to 24 inches high

---

[39] Snyder, 93.
[40] J. C. Powell to Maddry, February 20, 1938.

were completed and then allowed to thoroughly dry for 4 - 8 days before going higher. A man could then stand on the wall and trim it with a cutlass to give it a smooth facing. Building had to be done in the dry season to get the mud to harden. That was also when the men were freer from their farm work and could contribute their labor."[41]

Later the churches were built of concrete blocks and stucco. Those materials made them more resistant to the tropical rain and wind storms.

"The natives were afraid of climbing on ladders and scaffolding, so he invented a way of building the roof on the ground, and then, with a system of pulleys and a minimum of climbing, the roof would be lifted into place."[42]

One occasion brought tragedy to the building crew and the mission, but resulted in an opportunity to demonstrate Christian love to a Muslim family and community: "We're kept very busy these last few days. There's always plenty to do, but with the building there's more than usual. Daddy can scarcely get the carpentry work done ahead of the builders.

---

[41] Powell, *Impressions*, 93.
[42] Snyder, 93.

"On Saturday he hoped to breathe for a few minutes ... when the builder came up and announced the death of one of the laborers, caused by a big stone falling on him. Abiola had told them not to dig there. They did not listen and the stone came near getting seven or eight.

"We were so glad one of the boy's older brothers was working on the wall, and saw the accident. These two and others were from a Mohammedan home.

"Carl got busy and made a box. We lined it with white cloth. The body was put inside and the lid fastened on. It was carried to the home of the parents. Some of the father's older brothers witnessed the making of the box, putting the body in and sealing. They were satisfied, yes even gratified. So were the parents.

"The builders and a number of Christians went to take the body home and salute the parents. They found Mohammedan priests there ready to perform the last rites. They [wanted] to tear the box to pieces. The parents and relatives objected to this.

"We arrived in time to see the box put into the grave. The hole was very shallow, not much deeper than the box. They put many leaves inside and covered the box with mud balls. After that there was a Mohammedan prayer. We left. ...

"We are hoping that even though the boy died suddenly and tragically, that through this experience some members of the family understand a bit of Christianity and some points of difference between it and Mohammedanism. We pray that ultimately some of them may become Christians."[43]

If Carlyle brought sound building practices to the bush of Nigeria, he was also renowned for his ingenuity. A friend wrote in 1961, "Shakitown is still growing.... Fanfan stream will be dammed near Oze where Mr. Powell once built a bridge with old car chases."

### Evangelism and Church Starting

Not only did Carlyle work in building the buildings for churches and schools, he also was heavily involved in launching and supporting the groups of believers who would make up the congregations. "I know a church that was begun by some carriers that were talking with a farmer who happened to be standing by while these men were eating their

---

[43] Rosa Powell from Shaki to Mary Hester Powell, November 6, 1933.

noon day meal. I know another church that had its beginning by a man who was not even a member of a church. He had only heard a few Christian services, but decided to worship Jehovah. There being no Baptist church nearer than about twenty miles, he called all his friends together and explained what he knew about Christ. These people applied to me for our denomination to take over their guidance into faith and I helped them all I could, baptizing a few right away and teaching and guiding others along the way.

"Many places of worship were started by traders who stopped in a town that didn't have a place of worship. The traders would gather together with people in the village and have a worship service to Jehovah. Before long, the group would apply to us or to the traders' mother church for oversight and assistance. The mission always looked for strategic centers and placed people there. Sometimes it was to strengthen a work going on there. Sometimes it was to start one from scratch.

"In cases where a group of worshippers were attempting to get a church established, they would apply either to us or to some established church for assistance. Sometimes the mission would pay the native worker a very small remuneration for his work.

"As a rule it's important not to withdraw aid completely for a good many years as many of those places prove to need supervision even long after they are financially able to provide for themselves. I had one town in particular where the church paid all the salary for the pastor, but the mission continued to pay a portion of the school teacher's salary. The people themselves said they wanted the mission to keep paying just a little so the mission could keep its hand in the work."[44]

One time Carlyle told an American church he'd opened up a new area for the gospel at the point of a gun! He quickly added he'd killed a large animal and brought a large part of the meat to the chief of a village. Then he asked if he might be able to present the Gospel message. The chief granted him permission.[45]

There were huge numbers of baptisms - sometimes hundreds at a time - most in the river. Native lay preachers might draw folks to faith in Jesus Christ, but the missionary was the one who examined them as to their faith and baptized them.

---

[44] Powell, *Impressions*, 84-86.
[45] Notes prepared to introduce her father by Mary Hester Powell, no date.

## Teacher and Women's Worker

Rosa's role in mission work focused on women's work and on teaching. Rosa taught a total of 17 years including the two years in the US before her marriage. In the early years she was at Oyo mission station.

Upon their return from furlough in 1933, discussions began for the start of a new school in Shaki. The vision was for a school for older girls who needed exposure to Christian teaching to help them not only with their education but in resistance to the polygamy so rampant in the country.

Miss Elma Elam expressed an interest in launching the school in Shaki and Rosa and J. C. Powell agreed to relocate there from Oyo to further the work. The Baptist Iyawo ("Brides") School was launched April 17, 1934. Having no buildings of its own, they met in mission house number one. Elma Elam emerged as principle of the school.

Rosa and Elma's furloughs overlapped in 1940 and they tried to return together aboard the Zamzam. The ill fate of that ship delayed their arrival. In addition, Elma Elam suffered severe health issues and she died November 13, 1941 of a ruptured ulcer before being able to return to Nigeria.

Following Elam's death, Miss Hattie Mae Gardner became the school's second principal. Rosa continued teaching there until 1946 when she became principal at Oyo Baptist Boys' School. In 1942 the name of the school in Shaki was changed to Elam Memorial Iyawo School and later simply to Elam Memorial Baptist School. In 1959 the school celebrated its silver anniversary bringing together many alumnae, faculty and pastors and laying the cornerstone for a new dormitory. Hattie Gardner and Susan Anderson were both back for the celebration and each led one of the prayers.

Carlyle was able to continue as a field missionary from Shaki. His advisory and construction work never saw a pause. He also plunged into the construction of buildings at the new school. The first was dedicated in September, 1934. Other projects continued right through the war years as money and materials were available. After several years of struggle, the school was included in the Lottie Moon Christmas Offering in the early 1940s.

"We have found that education itself is one of the best means of introducing children and even adults to faith in Jesus Christ.

"Our schools had their beginning when a missionary at work in a station would gather a few children who happened to live nearby and teach them. As a rule, those children were not interested enough to come very far or stay very long. Many who did come did so very irregularly. Sometimes the missionary would actually have to pay them to come to school."[46]

Rosa furthered her education beyond the years at Meredith by attending the University of North Carolina at Chapel Hill in the summer of 1918. She continued to take classes during furloughs at the North Carolina College for Women (1927 and 1932).

Rosa was strong in prayer over large and small things. She often met a situation saying, "Let us pray over this."

Ethel Rebecca Harmon of Corbin, Kentucky, a fellow missionary to Nigeria, wrote for Rosa's service record: "The sun was never too hot nor the miles too long for her to reach the smallest village or church to give encouragement and help needed and to witness for her Lord."

---

[46] Powell, *Impressions*, 70-71.

## Established In the Work

The Powells' fast start in mission work was noted in Richmond. Ray wrote Carlyle: "I am very glad to get the news notes about the progress of your work in Oyo. You are certainly rendering a good account of yourself and I am happy to see you able to do as much work as you are at this stage of your missionary career. You speak like an old hand at the business."[47]

Nor was construction the only aspect of Carlyle Powell's work. His preaching and teaching combined with the effectiveness of the national pastors in their local work produced great results spiritually. Often he baptized large numbers - even in the hundreds - as national lay preachers and pastors also brought converts from their ministries to the missionary.

By the end of their second tour, both Carlyle and Rosa were taking on more and more responsibility. In a letter back home June 6, 1926, Carlyle talked about having taken on "church affairs" in both the Oyo and Shaki stations and how busy it made him.

The demands of missions abroad never have insulated missionaries from worries back

---

[47] March 3, 1921.

home. In 1926 the Bank of Warsaw failed due to employee fraud. Carlyle's father, Julius Alexander Powell, was on the bank board at the time. He and the rest of the board, scramble as they might to recover, could not bring the local institution back from the brink. Carlyle's sister, Annie Kate Powell, a sharp business woman despite her confinement to a wheelchair by childhood polio, managed the couple's money back in the states and had placed their meager savings in the Warsaw bank. That few dollars was gone, never to be recovered in those days before federal insurance of the banks. Carlyle wrote to console Annie Kate, telling her he would have put the money into the same bank had he been home.

The Powells launched their missionary careers at the best possible time for support from home. With the end of the Great War, there was a new sense of optimism. Joined with that was an even greater sense of responsibility to help in the religious reconstruction of the world following the war and to carry out global evangelization. B. C. Hening of North Carolina recommended at a Southern Baptist Convention that the denomination commit to raising $25,000,000 for foreign missions in five years. But when the recommendation came back from committee, it was to raise $75,000,000. Thus the Seventy-Five

Million Campaign was born as the first unified financial program ever undertaken by the Southern Baptist Convention.

Initial results of the Seventy-five Million Campaign exceeded all expectations. The Foreign Mission Board, accepting the mandate to greatly expand its mission efforts, sent more missionaries and expanded the number of mission fields and programs in existing missions. While the Seventy-Five Million Campaign eventually fell far short of expectations ($58.6 million reported in 1925), initial income reports were beyond projections. As a result, the Board was even more aggressive with new work and personnel. When moderations were set in place because the campaign had fallen short, the Foreign Mission Board already had programs and personnel in place which needed to be supported.

The collapse of the stock market in 1929 and the beginning of the Great Depression drastically impacted the income of the churches back home and therefore of the Foreign Mission Board. By 1932 the FMB was $1,110,000 in debt and sometimes suffering the embarrassment of not being able to service that debt.[48]

Carlyle Powell's early construction work occurred during the boom days of the 1920s. Letters exchanged between him and the FMB were filled with his requests for more money for building and support of national pastors and the regular fulfilling of those requests by the Board. The decade of the 1930s was just as equally austere.

Fire at the Foreign Mission Board long ago took the records of Carlyle and Rosa Powell for the years 1923-1932. It remains a gap in their service records and in the account of their service which family records and correspondence do not adequately fill. But the early years of their service establish a trajectory which is continued when the records resume in 1933.

---

[48] For coverage of the financing of the FMB during the period between the wars, see William R. Estep's <u>Whole Gospel Whole World</u>, 187-216.

**Carlyle Powell with other hunters**

## Chapter 8
## Life in Africa

*Inside the Powell House, covered in debris ... a heavy wooden table with a top perhaps two feet square ... an end table with a large, carved elephant supporting the top. In another place a smaller, stand alone, carved elephant. I would find a letter from Mary Hester Powell from the 1960s talking about her concern for the pieces as they were being shipped from Nigeria.*

Southwestern Nigeria is a tropical, savanna climate subject to some monsoons. There are only two variations in the climate – dry and wet. Temperatures can reach over 110 degrees in the wet season and annual rainfall along the coast reach well over 100 inches.

In the early 20$^{th}$ century, disease was rampant in that tropical climate. Those spending time in country were required to take daily doses of anti-malarial drugs. Family members reported the missionaries had to take five grams of quinine per day until they returned to the United States.

Standing water could not be trusted and had to be boiled. Rain water was sometimes caught from the roofs. Westerners had to boil water to be sure it was safe. There was no air conditioning or refrigeration. At one time the

Powells acquired a gas-powered refrigerator, but they rarely used it. Gas which was selling for 10-12 cents per gallon in the United States at the time was $1.50 in Nigeria.

In the Yoruba tribe, people lived in large family groups, often within one house. "All members of a family lived in one big, 'U'-shaped house which partly surrounded an open court. If a man took another wife, he would simply add to one end of the "U". Additions would be made as the family grew through additional wives or when sons married. I have seen whole villages of as many as 300-400 people made up of a single, huge house.

"The porch of the house stretched all the way around and faced the central, open space. The porches were wide enough to accommodate a person who chose to recline or sleep there. They also did most of their cooking in the open courtyard and food preparation was done on the porch. When houses were built, there was usually total disregard to neighboring homes or roads. Great holes dug randomly to obtain clay for building impeded both foot and vehicular traffic."[49]

---

[49] Powell, *Impressions*, 44-45.

Furnishings were sparse. Rounded, leather cushions called "tim-tims" served for seating.

The diet of the missionaries depended upon native foods and game but also included canned and dried items from the United States or Britain. "This time of year our food becomes meat and starches largely. ... We do not have much flour for cookies. ... Both of us are able to do full days' work and eat three square meals, so we have nothing to worry about as far as our health is concerned."[50]

Cooking was mostly from scratch. Most meals not only fed the missionaries, but a variety of local workers, school children and visiting national pastors and church leaders. As a result, there was often a national cook who prepared meals, even traveling with the missionaries as they visited distant villages. In one letter Rosa bemoaned the fact their cook was not very clean with the cooking utensils.

First marriages were arranged by parents and rarely included any courtship. Additional wives were taken by men or inherited from brothers or uncles. "Men strove to be wealthy. Wealth was gauged by the number of wives and children a man had. Marriage was not based upon love as best I

---

[50] Letter from Rosa Powell, April 27, 1947

could determine. The Alafin, or ruler of the people, had about 700 wives. A man would sometimes bargain for the girl as soon as she was born. Usually, however, the boy's father asked for the girl and bargained with her father until agreement was reached. The children would be married based not on courtship, but on contract.

"Most Yoruba fathers would engage their daughters before they reached the age of eight. The choice of suitor depended largely upon which boy's father made the highest offer. Some Western observers have gone so far as calling this "selling" of the children. While Yoruba fathers fiercely objected to that label, they would generally admit that monetary consideration had its influence upon their decision."[51]

" The custom of family marking by gashing or even removing slices of skin on their faces and sometimes on their arms and bodies was widespread and persistent through our whole tenure, particularly among those not associated with Christianity. I have seen as many as 1000 scars on one child. Their ears were pierced and ready for earrings almost from birth. Beads and chains around their

---

[51] Powell, *Impressions*, 47-48.

waists, wrists, ankles and necks were always worn and helped cover their nakedness."[52]

"Women did most of the carrying and marketing of produce. Women's heads were the means of transporting the goods to market. Men rarely carried produce on their heads. I have supposed the tradition arose during long periods of inter-tribal conflict when men found it necessary to carry bows and spears to protect the family as they traveled along to market."[53]

New missionaries to Nigeria in 1920 came at a time when the nation was still developing. There was little infrastructure. The necessities of life were hard to come by and expensive if bought. Hunting and farming were part of many missionaries' lives. If they had come from a farm family as both Rosa and Carlyle had, they not only could help provide food for themselves, but, with produce left over, for the village - that is if the garden could be protected from the many animals in and around the villages.

"Once while in Africa, he received a letter from a young seminary student asking advice on what to study, and what particular skills to acquire before going to Nigeria as a missionary. ...when his reply came, it said:

---

[52] Ibid., 55-56.
[53] Ibid., 54.

'Learn to build a decent chicken coop. You cannot bring a more valuable skill with you.'"[54]

"In the first years of their service, the trip to Africa was a long tedious journey by boat, with stopovers for as much as three weeks at a time in England, waiting to catch the next passenger boat around the coast of Spain and West Africa."[55]

"Later on, when they began to travel by plane, he said, 'I didn't trust that thing, and never did put part of my weight down on the seat. That is strong medicine. One drop will kill you.'"[56]

The road system in Nigeria in the early part of the twentieth century consisted of few paved roads and many dirt ones which became more poorly maintained as one got further from the main towns. Sometimes the missionaries had no automobiles (or "motors" as they called them, reflecting the British vernacular). When automobiles were available, many of the churches were far off the road and had to be reached by trail. Even into the later years of the family's mission service, hiking for miles was a necessity to reach the churches in more remote villages. "The needs in various

---

[54] Snyder, 93-94.
[55] Ibid., 92.
[56] Ibid., 93.

areas are calling, so we may take some bush trips."[57]

Obtaining gas was also a constant challenge, especially when world markets grew tight. "... in this country gas is either in your home or in the shop which in this case happens to be at least 19 miles away."[58]

Just getting from place to place within the country was a considerable challenge, but the results were often astounding: "During the first two weeks of October [1938] Rev. J. C. Powell and I, together with a number of native preachers, went to [the Ekiti Territory] to hold simultaneous revivals in each of the churches.... As the native preachers held revival services in the various churches, Mr. Powell and I went from church to church, holding all-day services, seeking to turn the people away from polygamy and other evil practices that have crept into the churches. ... On [a] Monday morning we set out for Ikogosi. The town is twelve miles from the road and it was necessary for us to walk the distance over a native bush path. ... Twelve Y.W.A. girls met us on the road to carry our loads to Ikogosi. They had walked the twelve miles before 9 o'clock that morning. As soon as they ate

[57] Rosa Powell to her mother, June 22, 1947.
[58] Rosa Powell to her sister and Mary Hester, September 7, 1935.

breakfast, they put our loads on their heads and started out in a brisk walk to Ikogosi. (Breakfast for the entire group cost less than 25 cents). When we were about two miles from the town the church members and their friends met us. There was about 500 people in the group. The school children carried a large banner telling us that we were welcome. ... After proper salutations they began to beat their native drums and to dance and sing.... When we came to the edge of town there were 21 native hunters lined up with their native guns to give us a royal salute. The entire crowd came into the large church building and gave us a welcome such as I had not seen before. After a brief service that afternoon, we urged all the people to return for the all-day meeting on the following day. The king and all his chiefs came and sat throughout the meeting. Although he and all his chiefs are heathen, he gave his full support to all the things we are trying to do. After the service they showered us with gifts of chickens, eggs, yams, fruit, etc. We announced we would pull teeth for anyone suffering with bad teeth. In a short while 65 bad teeth had been pulled. ... Early the next morning twelve other girls came to carry our loads back to the road. We then journeyed a few miles by car and had a similar service with another church that day."[59]

---

[59] A. C. Donath, Christmas letter of 1938.

Later, Rosa wrote about a bush trip she and "Carl" and Miss Young took. The couple had already walked an hour before they got to Miss Young. They had carriers with them for the gear and food, but the long walk was exhausting for both women. Both had blisters on their feet and a cut on one of Miss Young's feet because her shoe was worn completely through. It poured the rain and Rosa's raincoat was in one of the bundles with the carriers who were by then far ahead. The village to which they traveled was seven miles off the "motor road." When she wrote the letter they were stranded on a road near Okeho because rain had washed out the road. They were planning to sleep in the car. Despite the problems, Carl had baptized fourteen.[60]

When roads were present but the missionaries had no access to "motors," bicycles were an option. Carlyle and Rosa were both cyclists. Carlyle once rode from Oyo to Abeokuta without stopping.

Western missionaries were an unusual sight in some parts of the Nigerian bush. "We always had spectators when we were in, and particularly when we were eating. These curious bad boys cannot see well enough on the ground, so they climb into the trees nearby

---

[60] Rosa Powell to her sister and family, September 7, 1935.

and gaze with all the intensity of their being. Sometimes it becomes unbearable, and we choose the dark instead."[61]

Fear of the bush gradually gave way. Rosa wrote to Mary Hester they had been traveling in the bush to five outlying churches. None had pastors, being lay-led. Seats and pulpits were made of mud and bamboo or of wood only. "I slept that night in a building which had doors but no shutters for the windows, and strange to say I was not a bit afraid. Thick bush joined the edge of the compound not ten steps away, and different kinds of animals could have visited me, but I did not mind."[62]

Travel in the bush was an essential part of advancing the Gospel of Jesus Christ. Rosa wrote to Mary Hester she had traveled around Ajaiye to ten villages and spoken twenty times. "I could have visited in 40 more villages if time had been sufficient. In many of these there is not one Christian." (Letter from Shaki, May 7, 1935)

Superstition was a major and daily part of life for most of the Yoruba people and a constant concern for the missionaries who served them. On one occasion, when a pastor

---

[61] Rosa Powell to family, September 7, 1935.
[62] From Shaki, May 26, 1935.

was found to be a polygamist, his ordination papers were revoked. In anger and believing a fellow pastor had caused the revocation, the man sought to retaliate. "... so he has been going to Aha, a city ten miles from here, from one to six times a week since last Easter hiring a witch doctor to make medicine to run pastor Imosun out of town. Of course, the Juju man or witch doctor ... gets money for the job. Now he believes this man can have some mysterious power to make some substance seen or unseen, that will cast a spell over the pastor's mind and make him leave his people." In actuality, it was J. C. Powell, himself, who had caused the polygamist pastor to lose his ordination papers.

"Two weeks ago I was out at a small village near the Dahomey and some of the pastors came to me and told me there was a witch in town. She was a *shampanna* priestess or a woman who worships the origin of small pox. They make it their business to scatter the disease of small pox because as a priestess of this cult she gets the clothes of the dead person. They told me that there were over 50 children of the Christians of this town to die this year of small pox. They had this priestess up in court and [some of the officials] lied for her and the officers had not gotten back to Oyo before she was having a secret festivity over her victory in law. They all have the idea that she is a witch and they are scared to testify against her....

"These people believe they can wish a thing so strong until they can wish a boil or an ulcer or a cancer or an itching spot or a disease on their fellow man and it will come to pass." Carlyle described a man who found a wad of rags in the home of his mother who had died. He became convinced those rags were "medicine" cast on the departed woman and the cause of her death.

"Every hunter has his peculiar type of medicine. Some of them cake cold blood on the gun stock. [They believe] this makes the gun anxious to draw blood of the peculiar type of animal.... They most all of them wear a small gourd about the size of a hickory nut and it has blood out of the animal they wish to slip up on. When they wear this, [they believe] they become invisible, unsmellable, unhearable to the animal he is [hunting]." He also described a teacher at one of the schools asking for the entrails of a cobra so he could "make medicine" - an oil he intended to rub on the chest of his baby.[63]

Superstition is strongly akin to magic. Many of the practices of the Yoruba were

---

[63] J. C. Powell to Mary Hester Powell from Shaki, December 19, 1939.

efforts at modifying chance events or came from fear of and an effort to explain the unknown. "Margaret was whistling after supper tonight; and was promptly told that the Yorubas think that any woman who whistles is a witch! It seems ... that nobody ... is supposed to whistle during a rainstorm, because it may call the thunder!"[64]

The people looked for improvement in their lives. Where they saw it, they were quick to accept and acknowledge its apparent source. Often that worked to the advantage of evangelism. Christianity is, after all, a very practical faith asserting God intersects our lives. "We went back to see the old, old woman who had given up her image of the devil that she used in begging. She was most ardent in her praise of Jesus; said she's making a much better living, even as a beggar, than before she became a Christian."[65]

"The Yoruba also believed in the influencing power of magic. In Shaki, Christians were constructing a church inside of which a Mohammedan priest put paper bearing Arabic writing. When the laborers found the note, they refused to work because they believed the priest had used 'medicine' on

---

[64] Mary Hester Powell to David and Naomi Chambers, March 11, 1958.
[65] Mary Hester Powell to "folks," December 1, 1957.

them. On another occasion I saw a girl refuse to go home because she was afraid her mother would use 'medicine' to make her quit loving the man she wanted to marry."[66]

Local and family idols were common and a staple of indigenous worship. "The word *orisha* means 'things collected together.' My missionary colleague, Dr. George Green believed *orishas* involved ancestor worship. Our oldest native worker, Pastor Oyedato, said it conveyed to the Yoruba mind the idea of intercession between God and man and that the thing itself received and presented the sacrifice to God on behalf of the worshiper. Our most educated worker, Professor Nathaniel D. Oyerinde, who did graduate work at the University of Chicago, insisted Yoruba people usually have their own *orishas* and see themselves as the priests.

"An *orisha* may be on a hill or it may be the hill itself. They can be rivers, stones, brooks, pots, or strange groupings of articles. Always there is something extraordinary about the place or thing and evidence of sacrifice and worship. If the *orisha* was well kept, there was a path leading to it and an odd collection of things that appealed to Yoruba fancy.

---

[66] Powell, *Impressions*, ,13.

"The people set apart rooms in their homes or places scattered in their fields and in the woods. They built small houses for their idols in these places and sometimes on the street. I learned the names of 110 of these *orishas* and I believe the number of them could have gone beyond a thousand."[67]

Religion, even in strongly Christian Western Nigeria in the middle of the twentieth century, was divided roughly three ways between native cults, Muslim and Christian. Even as late as the 1952 census Christians were shown to be 37 percent of the population in the Western Region and Muslims were 33 percent. The Western region was the most densely Christian.

"During our stay in Nigeria, there was religious intolerance by Muslims wherever they had power and religious and political chicanery where they were in the minority. At Lagos and Sierra Leone it pursued peaceful propaganda because British authority would not allow a more direct persecution of its opponents.

"There was not a Yoruba town regardless how small which did not have its Mosque. In each of those towns from one to perhaps 50 imams daily called the faithful to

---

[67] Ibid., 39-40.

prayer. There were even many mosques and imams in Oyo although that was the seat of the *Alafin* or king who was considered the head of the Yoruba heathen religion. From one to five imams usually accompanied the *Alafin* to his farm. I never called upon any ruler of any city and stayed as much as fifteen minutes that one of the imams did not either walk by or come in and listen to the conversation. His actions clearly said 'Your Honor, I also am here with my religion.'"[68]

Rosa wrote Mary Hester, "this town had many Mohammedans, and they made the work difficult. They would stand at the windows and talk, and refuse to come inside when invited."[69]

There were times Muslim action crossed the line into persecution. "In July 1926, Rev. William Henry Carson with the Glee Club of the College and Seminary of Ogbomoso and I visited some of the churches in the Shaki district. When Muslims learned we had arrived, they immediately gathered in the streets in front of Christian homes and cried out "The god of the Christians is no God." They felt fairly safe if they created strife because the ruler of the town was in sympathy with them. After the concert, Christians reported three

---

[68] Powell, *Impressions*, 20.
[69] July 10, 1935.

times to me of being publicly insulted in the marketplace. ...

" In order to wedge his way into the confidence of a heathen, a Muslim would give or sell a clipping from the Koran written in Arabic. He would claim the text would bring good luck to the home and prevent evil spirits from entering and harming the occupants. Often those who held to traditional African beliefs would receive and value the gift as he would an *orisha*. His Muslim acquaintance would then present the Koran as the one set of written laws for his religious and moral life."[70]

Dress and home life were distinctive and regularly shocked Western sensibilities: "I've often been asked 'What is the form of native dress?' I have more than once answered 'The African style of dress is mostly "undressed."' But that's misleading. Actually, the forms were legion - especially among the Yorubas. Everyone's garment seemed to be cut to fit his own taste. With exceptions, one might say two pieces - shirt and trousers - constituted the dress for the men. Shirttails were almost always untucked and farmers often wore only trousers. Women wrapped around themselves a piece of dyed cloth very much like a bed sheet, but they began adding a waist shirt. Children were mostly nude.

---

[70] Powell, *Impressions*, 22.

"In addition to the costume, hair was dressed and trinkets and scars adorned the body. Ornamentation generally followed family traditions or were governed by religious belief."[71]

J. C. Powell was a hunter - both for food and for sport. " I have often been asked about the hunting in Africa. I hunted frequently both for recreation and because we and the native people in our mission compound could use the meat. Game was very plentiful. I would often take a double-barreled shotgun with one barrel loaded for shooting fowl and the other for shooting deer. During my first three-year tour, I killed 63 deer. Larger and predatory game we seldom hunted and elephants not at all. Elephants were scarce in Nigeria even then and the government required a $225 license to take one - an enormous amount of money for that day."[72]

Carlyle wrote Mary Hester about his hunting exploits: "You just ought to have seen your Daddy not long ago when I went out with Dr. Anders and killed a buffalo. My, your old dad was strutting around like a Bantam rooster."[73] In addition to hunting for food,

---

[71] Ibid., 9-10.
[72] Ibid., 15-16.
[73] From Shaki, April 1, 1934.

Carlyle Powell found recreation in target practice during those rare times when his busy missionary schedule permitted.

There were dozens of little things that challenged or shaped the lives of the Powells as well as other missionaries. Consider how hard it must have been to be paid in U. S. dollars by the Foreign Mission Board but live in a British province where everything was priced in Pounds Sterling. Mary Hester moaned in one of her letters that filing income tax took three times as long.

While on furlough, Carlyle wrote a letter in which he mentioned he was having problems writing at night. He was in Burgaw at the time and the train was sounding its air horn.[74] He'd become accustomed to the quiet of the Nigerian nights.

---

[74] September 3, 1940.

**Mary Hester Powell baby picture**

## Chapter 9
## Then There Were Three

*Among the myriad photographs, a black and white one of a little girl in a dress and hat standing in the dirt driveway to a house with a palm tree in the background - Mary Hester Powell at her Oyo home.*

### The First White Child

Mary Hester Powell was born May 21, 1922 in Oyo, Nigeria. "Mary Hester was the first white child ever born in the Yoruba Tribe. They gave her a special name, 'Abe Au Se,' meaning 'Born on Sunday.' When her mother carried her out in the carriage, the natives would follow in droves just to get a peep at her, for, until then, the only white people they had seen were adults."[75]

Only a few days after Mary Hester was born, Carlyle made a kill of two or three antelope - far more meat than they could use. He suggested they give a feast for the school boys who helped around the farm. "It happened that the feast was held the day Mary Hester was eight days old. It was an old traditional Yoruba custom to hold a feast on the eighth day honoring a new birth. The boys never knew it was meant for them. They came

---

[75] Snyder, 95.

bringing gifts and saluted her. They were so grateful to him for carrying out their custom."[76]

When she was four months old, proud Papa wrote to T. B. Ray at the Foreign Mission Board, "Our little baby is doing fine. She is getting now where she is noticing everything she hears and sees. Growing nicely. Weighs about 13 1/2 or 14 lbs now."[77] One has to imagine the uncertainty of caring for an infant as first-time parents and in an underdeveloped country half a world from family and friends. Only then can one understand the relief they must have felt when their baby was thriving.

That did not mean raising a baby in developing Nigeria was without challenge. "Mary Hester ... has had fever since I wrote, and I am still giving her double doses of Quinine. She is the busiest baby you ever saw. One day last week she made starch - wasted ... more than enough for one whole week's washing." Mary Hester was four.[78]

---

[76] Ibid.

[77] J. C. Powell T. Bronson Ray, Executive Secretary of the Foreign Mission Board, September 10, 1922.

[78] Rosa Powell at Oyo to Annie Kate Powell, June 6, 1926.

## Furloughs

The typical rotation of missionaries involved a three-year service period on the field followed by a year in the United States. That furlough year was important to the health of missionaries, especially those who were laboring in tropical, disease infested regions like Nigeria of the early twentieth century. Sometimes it took the whole year of furlough to get the missionaries' health back to a level that could sustain another tour abroad.

Nor were missionaries idle during the furlough year. The Foreign Mission Board expected them to rest and recuperate for a period of several weeks. After that they were permitted and even encouraged to accept speaking engagements at churches and lead and speak at the more regional schools of missions. The traveling was called "deputation" work and was one of the main ways the Foreign Mission Board built awareness of mission needs among the churches. Missionaries handled their own appointment schedules and travel arrangements.

Without the support of "mission boards," missionaries spent and still spend those stateside months actually raising funds for their mission efforts. Prior to the beginning of the Cooperative Program in 1925, even Southern Baptist missionaries were more hands-on in raising their funding, although such funding was generally directed through the Foreign Mission Board.

The Cooperative Program was an agreement among the boards and agencies and with the authorization of the Southern Baptist Convention by which they abandoned most of the direct efforts of supporting their work. For the missionaries, it meant stopping the solicitation of pledges of support and donations from churches. Instead, regular giving to the Cooperative Program by local churches was intended to fund foreign, home and state missions as well as the seminaries and agencies of the SBC.

"The spring she was five, the Powells were due to come back to America on furlough. Her grandfather had bred his cows so there would be ample good, fresh milk for his granddaughter; and Mamie [a cousin ten years older than Mary Hester] who always thought ice cream was the epitome of elegance, had saved her nickels to treat her to ice cream cones. Both were slated for disappointments.

"At supper the first night, Mary Hester looked up and said, 'Mother, do you suppose they have any "tinned milk"? I don't like this.'

Canned milk was all they could get in Africa and on the ship.

"The next morning, Mamie could not wait to carry her to the drug store for her first ice cream cone. She took one bite and said, 'No, it is too cold.'"[79]

"When Mary Hester was about eight.... One day, [her father] heard a conversation in the courtyard. Although he could not understand it all, he caught enough to realize that someone was really being chewed out, and Mary Hester was doing it. He slipped to the door and listened. He realized that the boys had done something of which Mary Hester disapproved, and she was telling them off in no uncertain terms. He said then that she had a better command of the language than he had. He declared that the Yoruban language was a child's language. You could not learn it in a classroom, but had to learn it from hearing it spoken."[80]

## Depression Years

The Cooperative Program had not long been around when the leanest days of the Great Depression hit the world and the Foreign

---

[79] Snyder, 96.
[80] Ibid., 95.

Mission Board along with it. The Mission Board, already in debt even during the better days before the Depression, found itself unable to pay its bills, support the budgets of the various missions around the world and even to pay the travel and salaries of the missionaries.

Several of the missionaries who returned home on furlough during the 1930s found themselves unable to return to the field because the Board could not afford to pay their travel expenses. Rosa and Carlyle Powell found themselves in just such straits in 1932.

In their first three tours in Nigeria, resources had flowed easily through the Foreign Mission Board to the fields. Those pre-Depression days were good days in the U. S. Over and over Carlyle would make huge budget requests for expansion and construction. Over and over he would hear from Richmond the entire budget had been approved.

But the Depression years brought a total change on the mission field. Contributions to the churches back home and to the Foreign Mission Board fell off dramatically. The Foreign Mission Board itself went into debt to keep the barest mission efforts afloat.

Carlyle, Rosa and Mary Hester returned to the United States on furlough in July 1931. Little did they know that furlough would be extended until May 1933 - double the normal one year. There simply was not enough money to send them back to Africa. The crisis fell not only on the Powells, but on some 30 missionaries stuck in the homeland because the mission board could not afford the travel expenses of returning them to the field. They were on indefinite furlough and even their salaries were not paid during those extended months.

Letters were sent from Carlyle to T. Bronson Ray, then Executive Secretary of the Foreign Mission Board, insisting they needed to return to Africa. Ray was reluctant to express the depth of the crisis, but finally wrote: "My dear fellow I hate to write you what I am compelled to write you, but I am compelled to say that I am afraid we are not going to have money with which to return you any time soon." Receipts by the mission board were down 25 percent for 1932. "It looks to me like we are right up against the necessity of marking time for a year or two."[81]

Carlyle wanted to raise his own funds to return to the field. But the Cooperative Program required an iron-clad policy

---

[81] T. Bronson Ray to J. C. Powell, May 5, 1932.

prohibiting missionaries from raising their own funds. If an individual or church offered funds on their own, the gift might be accepted. But the missionaries were banned from making any request of funds.

The exception to the policy of allowing missionaries to accept unsolicited donations led to considerable confusion. A flurry of letters between Carlyle and Ray over a period of more than a year were laced with frustration. Individual cases were reviewed, some funds accepted, many more situations discouraged or turned down as against policy.

The situation only grew worse during the winter of 1932-1933. "I am hoping and praying for one month when we will show a decided upward trend. Then I will begin to believe that the depression is passing."[82]

"The status of the income of the Foreign Mission Board makes us exceedingly uneasy about the work this year. Unless things improve very much in the near future, we are going to have to call home other missionaries and retrench in other ways undreamed of."[83]

---

[82] Charles E. Maddry to J. C. Powell, January 17, 1933. Maddry had taken office as Executive Secretary of the Foreign Mission Board October 12, 1932.
[83] Charles E. Maddry to J. C. Powell, January 26, 1933.

Eventually funding did come for the Powells' return to Africa. It came from a woman who was apparently among the sizable number of Southern Baptist laypersons who voluntarily underwrote costs of specific missionaries. "When you write Mrs. Brown salute her for me. I surely appreciate her sending us back." [84]

## Family Divided

Rosa had started teaching Mary Hester at home when she was very young. Mary had also had some opportunity to go to school with other missionary kids. On furlough back in North Carolina, Mary was enrolled in public school in the fifth grade, even though she was only nine.

As the missionary family prepared to finally return to the field in 1933, Carlyle and Rosa asked Mary Hester very directly if she wanted to return with them to Africa and continue her education there under her mother and the missionary kids' school. She chose to remain in the United States to get her education.

Rosa and Carlyle left her with the Hocutt family in Ashton. There Mary Hester

---

[84] J. C. Powell to Charles Maddry, January 1, 1934.

had her grandmother Hocutt and aunts still around the home place to guide and protect her. Other of her aunts and uncles were little older than she, since Rosa was the oldest of a very large brood of Hocutt children.

In Ashton she had to learn a new way of life - new people, new schedule, even different foods. Mary Hester commented in her older years her aversion to collard greens came from taking collard sandwiches to school. Perhaps some Down East foods were stranger than Nigerian foods.

This was also the beginning of Carlyle and Rosa sending half of their salary to Warsaw. It helped with Mary Hester's expenses and built up a little bank balance for emergencies. It was also drawn upon for purchases made in the States to be sent to Nigeria. Annie Kate Powell, Carlyle's sister, usually managed that money.

Most of the time Mary Hester Powell has used her first or both first and middle names. Friends and family stateside occasionally addressed her with the nick-name "Hess." Frequent letters were all that could keep parents and daughter connected while Mary Hester was back in the United States for her education. Letters from Nigeria, at first, were news from home for Mary Hester. Rosa wrote with some formality and signed all her letters "Mother." Carlyle carried on with nonsense and would concoct greetings for her.

"Dear Chicken Gizzard,  The last time I wrote to you I think I was in the horse pistol[85] at Ogbomoso, with my old leg torn wide open. Well it is well, but of course the place is tender and will always be a scar there, but all of the leg is still there and functioning fairly well."[86] He would also get very warm with her in his letters, calling her "Baby Girl."

For Carlyle and Rosa, the Nigerian children who thronged the churches and mission must have brought some relief of the loneliness of being away from their own daughter. "It may interest you to know that we now have fourteen young sons in our household. Where the parents cannot furnish part of the money, we take food towards their expenses. It makes my work heavier, because I must plan their meals so as to see that the food is not wasted, but I am enjoying it so far. ... By the time I have admitted them, boiled off their clothes, registered them in the school, and supplied them with books, I've been ready to

---

[85] Yes, Carlyle Powell actually wrote "horse pistol," referring, of course, to the hospital. Word play was always part of his humor.
[86] J. C. Powell at Shaki to Mary Hester Powell, October 30, 1933.

quit. In addition I try since Christmas to go into the school and spend the A.M."[87]

The attention from the native boys and even adults could also become invasive and annoying. "Aloke is trying to help the women to understand that Christianity means more than attending church or following their husbands to church. One unpleasant feature ... is ... being a monkey in a cage, in other words, being on exhibition for the benefit of satisfying their curiosity. We really had to close our windows and doors to keep from being gazed upon all the time we were eating or dressing. ... If they were anxious to know anything about Him we would be more patient with their curiosity. But mention the matter to them, and many times they laugh at you."[88]

## A New Normal

Once back in Nigeria, the Powells found everything changed. Money that had flowed freely from America in the pre-depression years had dried up. Gone were the meager salaries for builders to construct schools and

---

[87] Rosa Powell to Mary Hester Powell at the Hocutt house, February 11, 1934.

[88] Rosa Powell at Shaki to Mary Hester Powell describing their work at new outstations where the Christian message and white missionaries were a novelty, November 11, 1934.

churches. Even salary supplements for national pastors and teachers were almost all gone and would not recover in meaningful ways for several years.

Curtailment of building projects meant Carlyle could spend more time in the churches and at associational meetings, discipling and training the people and the pastors who served them. He began doing more teaching. It was Carlyle who would venture into the bush for weeks at a time, traveling with carriers of supplies and clothes to villages with no developed roads and little contact with the outside world.

Rosa and Carlyle along with other mission personnel would teach in many Bible Schools that could bring hundreds of children and adults for days and even weeks. Curriculums were more than Bible stories. Rosa described one: "Miss Elam taught 'The Plan of Salvation,' Daddy taught the Bible, Miss Victoria taught WMU Methods and Soul Winning, Alaki taught Child Welfare in Shaki, while Segilola did so in Okeho, and I taught Reading and Writing."[89]

Regular Bible Schools held at the village churches, even those back in the bush, would bring out hundreds of children. They were

---

[89] Rosa Powell to Mary Hester Powell, September 11, 1934.

regularly taught in the schools associated with the churches and during the schools' regular sessions. The attendance at such schools grew and grew until Rosa could report in 1946 that one school had an attendance of 1050. That year Miss Ethel Rebecca Harmon, a missionary, was making her rounds doing nothing but helping station personnel and national teachers lead Bible Schools.[90]

Carlyle wrote Maddry they had come back to live in a mission house that had been unoccupied for two years. He found the floors in their house eaten by white ants. He would have to replace several floorboards and a couple "sleepers."

"Some of the work has been crippled on account of insufficient funds, but I have a long time ago made up my mind not to grieve over what is lost, but to pick up the thread where I find it and weave the best I can regardless of the conditions I meet."[91]

The Depression tours of service for the Powells, 1933-1936 and 1937-1940, were carried out from Shaki whereas the earlier years had been in Oyo. Construction was not as intense because of lacking funds. But there continued to be expansion of the work.

---

[90] Rosa Powell to Mary Hester Powell, July 2, 1946.
[91] J. C. Powell to Charles Maddry, June 11, 1933.

Rosa wrote to Mary Hester they'd had guests at Shaki - Misses Young, Anderson and Dr. and Mrs. MacLean. She said Carl had to build bridges for them to drive in. "Miss Young christened her beautiful new Chevrolet on that trip."[92]

Mission budgets globally were pared back by the Foreign Mission Board as they tried to pay themselves out of debt. Repeatedly Carlyle would mention items the board had covered that were now left out of the budget. The most difficult was when the tiny salaries of the national pastors were eliminated. The salaries were only a few dollars a month for each man, but even that was beyond the Depression-era budgets of the Board.

Carlyle wrote to Maddry on New Years Day 1934 that he and Rosa had decided to cover the native salaries in their town from their own compensation. "...it will probably take a fifth of our little salary to meet these ... obligations the board has been carrying."

In the same New Years Day letter the results of the mission work was underscored. "During the last two months we have baptized 49 at Okeho and Oyo.... This is the best

---

[92] Rosa Powell to Mary Hester Powell, October 30, 1933.

prepared bunch of candidates I have ever examined...." Baptisms were regular and in rather large numbers. On another occasion, he reported he had just returned from a trip to Oyo where he baptized 40.[93]

As always, the lostness of the people was a constant heaviness on the hearts of the Powells. "They do not realize that they are sinners and that they are lost. Salvation to them means coming to church.... It is difficult to help them understand otherwise."[94]

Health issues constantly cropped up around all missionaries in Western Africa. In the summer of 1934, Mary Hester had her tonsils out back in the States. But in Nigeria, the concern was more menacing. Rosa wrote from Shaki that one of the boys in their school might have leprosy. If his tests turned out positive, he would have to spend a year in the leper colony at Ogbomoso. "Dr. Lockett started the colony and the medical authorities are very pleased with the entire project. ... We are not uneasy about getting it ourselves. If we should worry about such, you and we would have been dead long ago."[95] In January of that year Rosa had written that Mrs. Duval in Ogbomoso had small pox, and in March that

[93] J. C. Powell to Charles Maddry, March 30, 1939.
[94] Rosa Powell to Mary Hester Powell, October 2, 1934
[95] Rosa Powell to Mary Hester Powell, June 6, 1934.

one of the girls at their school had come down with it.

By the end of 1935 letters exchanged between Carlyle and Maddry were upbeat. The debt of the Foreign Mission Board had been reduced from $1.1 million to $485,000. All 30 missionaries who been on indefinite furlough were back on the field and 44 new missionaries had been appointed.

Carlyle was also writing Maddry they had asked folks back home to send Mary Hester to Campbell College for the spring. The change was apparently to spare her long bus rides necessitated in her current arrangements. Carlyle noted that even though Mary Hester was not in college yet (only 13), she was ahead of her years.

Rosa and Carlyle had another furlough during 1936 - 1937 giving them a chance to spend lots of time with Mary Hester. Carlyle spoke at a local Baptist Church in Buies Creek, the location of Campbell College, as one of his deputation appearances. The invitation was for mission service at home or abroad. Over 20 Campbell students responded.[96]

Mary Hester attended Buies Creek Academy (now Campbell University) 1934-38.

---

[96] News item in *Creek Peebles*.

She graduated high school at 16. Home and missionary schooling had given her a head start and she continued to be advanced. She also had some of her parents' athletic ability. While in high school she played basketball.

She continued her education at her mother's alma mater, Meredith College (now University), graduating in 1942. There she played tennis, was in the literary society, college choir, glee club and Baptist Student Union.

How can parents provide guidance to a teenaged daughter half-a-world away? When boyfriends began to be mentioned, both Carlyle and then Rosa wrote her to be cautious. Her mother thanked her for her openness about her men friends, then urged her to pray and follow the guidance of the Lord. "In the meantime, be kind to all, but intimate with none."[97]

In the same letter, she addressed another area where guidance was needed - in selection of a major in college and career decisions looming on the horizon . "I would suggest you take all the Bible you can get during your stay there. That is one subject that will do you good no matter what may be your calling in life. It will help you in any field of

---

[97] Rosa Powell to Mary Hester Powell, July 16, 1939

service you may enter. You cannot know it too
well."

Even much earlier, Rosa had given
Mary Hester freedom to select any course of
study, but with one stipulation: "Remember
this always - that so long as you attend to your
health physically, and are considerate of those
with whom you are living, we do not object to
your learning anything which will make you a
more efficient servant of the Master."[98]

## Ibarabas

The Great Depression had forced the
Foreign Mission Board into debt and
necessitated extremely limited budgets for all
mission work. At the same time the
government in Nigeria was requiring teachers
in mission-related schools to have more
credentials and training. "There is as much
difference in our work here now and what it
was five years ago as there is in eating chalk
and cheese."[99]

Demands on the missionaries increased
in part because there were calls for work to be
done in the northern areas. They went to Jos in

---

[98] Rosa Powell at Shaki to Mary Hester Powell at the
Hocutt house in Ashton, June 17, 1934
[99] J. C. Powell to Charles Maddry, February 20, 1938.

1939. Rosa wrote to Mary Hester their purpose in being there was to minister to Yoruba who had come there to live and work. That area was part of the Hausa tribe. It was another culture shock as Rosa reported the villagers rarely wore clothes at all, but only bunches of leaves as loin covering.

They found at Jos a weak church. The Yoruba Christians who were attempting to launch the church felt compelled to send money regularly to their mother church in southwestern Nigeria to help them pay for their church and school.[100]

A wider field of work was complicated by sometimes unreliable transportation. Rosa reported in one letter that Carl had taken the "motor" to the shop with a broken axle. "We would not spend money repairing it, but we must have something to use until we go home, since we are supposed to cover three associations." She went on to say they had walked between 15 and 18 miles one day because they didn't have the "petrol" to take them.[101]

In 1935 Carlyle wrote to Maddry he had the opportunity to go into a more northerly province and serve among the small tribe of

---

[100] Rosa Powell to Mary Hester Powell, July 24, 1939.
[101] Rosa Powell to Mary Hester Powell, October 5, 1939.

the Ibarabas. He asked for money for that effort even if it meant reducing the budget for the southern stations. "...we are the one denomination that reaches up to this tribe, and the others are looking to us to enter. I am the first man to get a site in this tribe."[102] Maddry replied that additional missionaries were being appointed and he was enthusiastic about the new tribe.[103] By February of the next year, Carlyle was writing he had the roof on the chapel/school building for the Ibarabas.[104]

"I was happy to secure land in the Ibaribos tribe for a school a few weeks ago. We have been hammering at this task for fifteen years. ... I was the first white man to secure land for a mission site in this tribe."[105]

Work among the Ibarabas did take hold and this tribe just to the north of Shaki became a mission focus of Yoruba churches. A quarter century later, Missionary Bonnie Moore wrote the Powells: "One home mission couple, Yorubas, working with the Ibaraba people... have taken several small children and babies into their home in order to keep their parents from killing them or giving them to another tribe as slaves. There is strong tribal prejudice

---

[102] J. C. Powell to Charles Maddry, July 11, 1935.
[103] Charles Maddry to J. C. Powell, August 26, 1935.
[104] J. C. Powell to Charles Maddry, February 8, 1936.
[105] J. C. Powell to Charles Maddry, June 11, 1935.

among the Nigerians and when you find a couple of one tribe taking in outcasts from another tribe, then truly we know it is because they have Christ in their hearts.... These children are killed or given into slavery because they cut their teeth at the wrong time! and it is their belief that if the parents keep them something bad will happen to the parents or in the village. Two of the Ibaraba boys who have become Christians and have learned how to read and write are planning to enter one of our schools this month. They want to learn more of Jesus so they can be better prepared to go back and witness to their people and 'tell them the Jesus way!'"[106]

### Health

Health issues arose during the mid-1930s. Rosa gave everyone a health scare in 1936: "Mrs. Powell is just at this time struggling along with her middle change of life and has been in bad health since the first of November. It struck like a storm. She has been over in Ogbomaso [sic] where Dr. Long could attend to her. She is now in Oyo with me and is planning to go on back to Shaki as I go. However she is going to have to go easy for awhile until she can wade through this."[107]

---

[106] Bonnie Moore to J. C. and Rosa Powell, January 1959.
[107] J. C. Powell to Charles Maddry, February 8, 1936.

Rosa's problems continued during the 1936-1937 furlough. She was hospitalized briefly in Wilmington. A single radium treatment was administered in an attempt to return her to health.

Correspondence with the Foreign Mission Board indicated some doubt she would be able to return to the field on time: "...the climatic conditions and the taking of quinine daily during the menopause is sometimes quite serious".[108]

Rosa wrote back to Jessie R. Ford who was coordinating the doctors and executives at the Board: "Now Miss Ford, I understand fully what the daily dose of quinine means." She went on to assure Ford she had experienced no ill effects from the quinine before. She knew people needed her in Africa. But she concluded her letter assuring that she would follow the advice and direction of the doctors and the Board.[109] In fact, her health improved so she could make the crossing.

If health was beginning to be an issue, it did not show up in the way they carried out

---

[108] Foreign Mission Board to Rosa Powell, March 13, 1937.
[109] Rosa Powell to Jessie Ford at the Foreign Mission Board, March 22, 1937.

their mission work. "... Carl and I spent a most enjoyable ten days visiting farm churches - which required walking almost daily ... eight to eighteen or twenty miles .... We had good meetings, received hearty welcomes, were bountifully blessed with good weather ... and were so conscious of the presence and power of the Holy Spirit every minute of the time. I enjoyed it more than any work I've had any part in during our stay on the field since 1920."[110]

It was Easter Sunday, March 24, 1940. Rosa wrote to Mary Hester she'd been to the leper colony in Oyo. Nineteen people had gathered. Two were baptized believers. Nine were seeking to follow Christ. Almost as an aside she noted they'd had their first convert from among the Ibarabas tribe.

Mary Hester Powell was always an obedient, grounded child. The same was true as a young woman. But one occasion brought her father to intervene emphatically. She wrote her parents in early 1940 asking if they objected to her going to prom. A flaming letter came back from "Sky" Powell: "Most emphatically yes. I do object to your ever playing the wild. ... I would not have married any woman in the world who was a dancer. ...

[110] Rosa Powell in Shaki to sister-in-law Annie Kate Powell, October 29, 1939.

If [boyfriend by name] is a dancer you better look for someone who has higher ideals of a woman's character." There followed a whole page, single-spaced, typed against dancing and "public hugging."[111]

Mary Hester was much missed in Nigeria. "I saw Adekonis - the big boy - a bit lame - who used to care for you when you were two or three years old. He took you to and from church in his arms many times. He calls you his child and begged for one of your pictures when I showed them to him. These people still love you, ask when you will be through school, and if and when you will be coming back to Nigeria. I tell them I do not know - that you and God will have to decide that."[112]

As Mary Hester reached young adulthood she clearly recognized the richness of her relationships with her Hocutt and Powell extended family. She sent a Mother's Day telegram on May 10, 1941 to her grandmother Powell and her Powell aunts living at the Powell house in Warsaw: "Love to you who have been like mothers to me." It was the single time in her life when she most

---

[111] J. C. Powell at Shaki to Mary Hester Powell, January 23, 1940.
[112] Rosa Powell to Mary Hester Powell at Meredith, February 16, 1940

needed the support of all those around her. Rosa was missing.

**Baptist Boys' High School**
**Oyo, Nigeria**
**Rosa Powell - center**

# Chapter 10
# The Zamzam

*I'd never heard of the* Zamzam. *Right away I learned from clippings in family genealogy of the ill-fated Atlantic crossing that almost turned tragic for its missionary passengers.*

From April 11, 1940 until March 15, 1941 Carlyle and Rosa Powell were in the United States on furlough. Mary Hester was in college at Meredith. Carlyle and Rosa split their time between the Hocutt family in Burgaw and the Powell family in Warsaw.

Word came to Carlyle that a sudden vacancy in Nigeria required his return to assume responsibilities until the vacancy was filled. He was able to get passage on a cattle ship, but Rosa had to stay behind for a few more days before she could leave to join him.

Missionary families become accustomed to being separated, especially when the children are back in the States in school. That is exacerbated when there is a crisis.

Passage was hard to obtain in those war years. While the United States was not yet in the war, the Atlantic had become a very dangerous water to cross. German U-boats and raiders were constantly on the prowl.

Named for a sacred well in Mecca, the *Zamzam* was an 8,000 ton cruise ship of Egyptian registry. Though the history of the ship was not generally known, it had been originally christened the *H. M. S. Leistershire* in 1910 and served during World War I as a troop transport under the British admiralty. Following its brief military history, the ship had been renamed and spent a number of years bearing Muslim pilgrims on their way to Mecca.

On March 20, 1941 it pulled away from Hoboken, New Jersey with 321 passengers and crew. Rosa Powell was one of the 201 passengers. There were 142 American passengers, 120 of them missionaries like Rosa, from 21 different denominations. In addition there were 24 ambulance drivers not actually enlisted in any military but going to provide aid to war casualties. In the cargo hold were 20 of their ambulances. Another six of the passengers were tobacco men - buyers and auctioneers, on their way to make inroads into the African tobacco market.

Passengers felt little danger. America was still a neutral country in the war. The *Zamzam* was a neutral ship. Furthermore, the ship's route had been intentionally plotted to avoid the U-boat filled North Atlantic. "That the ZamZam would receive its orders from the

British Admiralty, that it would travel in blackout, and that it would carry contraband, we did not know at the time of our departure from the States. ... She traveled in radio silence, flew no flag and had no identifying marks on her sides."[113]

Not long after they embarked, a couple of the passengers noticed there were not enough life jackets aboard. When the crew seemed unwilling to correct the situation, they reported it to the harbor police at a stop in Baltimore. The police refused to let the ship depart until additional life jackets were procured. That intervention turned out to be a life-saving action.

Though the ship had been billed as a luxury liner, passengers soon found it was anything but luxurious. Some recounted a poorly trained Egyptian crew who seemed to care little about Western desires for clean linen and food hardly up to cruise standards. An unusually cold March made the passengers uncomfortable and one even reported steam pipes which froze prior to departing on the journey south. They had assumed the ship was neutral by virtue of its registration in Egypt. Perhaps authorities encouraged that thought.

---

[113] Sylvia M. Oiness; *Strange Fate of the Zamzam: The Miracle Ship*; Minneapolis: Nathaniel Carlson, 1942; 8-9.

In fact, it was connected with the British admiralty.

The many missionaries aboard were all on their way to Africa. Though they were of many denominations, there was a fellowship among them that made it a unique trip if only for that reason. The American ambulance drivers, on their way to serve British and Free French forces in Africa, spent much of their time drinking in one lounge. The missionaries held prayer meetings with much singing.

The route of the ship was to take it to South America, then across the Atlantic to Capetown, South Africa and up the East coast of Africa to Mombasa, Kenya and finally to its home port of Alexandria. They left Recife, Brazil on April 9, 1941.

Before the ship left, Rosa wrote a letter to Mary Hester on April 6 in which she spoke of the bad conditions on the ship. "Certainly we must have some soap. Very little has been furnished us thus far, and it is like laundry soap. ... The blackout is a bit uncomfortable at times especially since our fan will not work at this particular time. ... Miss Elam just told me something interesting. She said she saw our table steward take the spoons we had used for grapefruit and give them to the O'Neal's[114]

---

[114] J. Paul and Meta LaTuille O'Neal.

without washing them. He gave them to us out of his pockets this morning. ...you see what their idea of sanitation is."

She wrote another letter to Annie Kate Powell. At the top of the letter she noted she was writing it from the *Zamzam*. It was dated April 7, but the postmark was April 10. The mail had obviously gone out just before the ship sailed: "The time on board has not seemed as long as it did the first few days out of Baltimore. Really for several days I was sick.... I felt I could not endure to look at the voyage ahead of me. However after those few days I've gotten along very well and don't worry so much about what is ahead of us. ... You know, I've traveled by water so much that everything seems so commonplace I feel there's not enough news to justify a 5 cent postage stamp - to say nothing of air mail postage."

The crossing became more serious when the crew painted all the windows black and they began running under total blackout conditions at night. A sudden change of course back toward South America was explained as an effort to avoid a suspicious ship reported in the area.

At dawn on April 17 many of the passengers of the *Zamzam* were still sleeping when the infamous German raider *Atlantis,* also known as *Tamesis,* began shelling from a distance of three and one-half miles. One of the shells took out the radio antennae. "A German official told us later that had our operator sent out a message for help, the raider would have torpedoed and sunk us immediately with no trace."[115]

A total of 55 shells were fired, nine striking the *Zamzam.* Pumps kept the liner afloat until passengers and crew were loaded into lifeboats. One of the lifeboats was obviously unfit for the water having been hit directly in the shelling. Two or three others were either riddled with shrapnel and soon sank or capsized when launched. As a result many passengers in life jackets ended up in the water.

The captain of the *Zamzam,* himself British and whose name passengers learned was "William Grey Smith", consigned all his documents and charts to the ocean. In the many, many accounts from survivors the crew of the *Zamzam* received little if any praise and were often accused of looking only to their own survival. The passengers were, however, unusually orderly and quiet for the circumstances. Those ambulance drivers sprang to action immediately to treat the injured.

---

[115] Oiness, 14.

Many of the missionary survivors viewed it as nothing short of a miracle there was no immediate loss of life. Though ten were injured, three seriously and one would eventually die of injuries, "Not one [of the missionaries] was injured in any way...."[116]

Before long, the raider came alongside. The German crew, armed with machine guns, lined the deck ready for any eventuality. Amidst that terrifying seizure, passengers of the *Zamzam* remembered seeing a rainbow arch across the morning sky - a singular cause of hope. The Powell family tradition said Rosa was the last passenger to leave the *Zamzam*.

The crew and passengers of the *Zamzam* were all plucked from the water. Small children were hoisted by baskets at the ends of long ropes. Adults and older children climbed rope ladders on the side of the raider.

The survivors soon found themselves treated almost like guests by the captain and crew of the raider. The German crew brought clothing and other supplies from the *Zamzam* and, some with tears in their eyes, tried to see to the comfort of their new prisoners. They were assured they would get their luggage and personal items back. In fact, though the

---

[116] Oiness, 13.

German sailors were seen making multiple trips to and from the *Zamzam* as it floundered, the passengers would get little of their belongings back at all. They could only assume the German crew kept most of it for themselves.

The captain of the *Atlantis*, they learned, was named Rogge and was a Lutheran. That Lutheran affiliation might have been very fortunate since a large number of the missionaries from the *Zamzam* were also Lutheran from the Augustana Synod in Minneapolis. The captain explained when they saw the *Zamzam* sailing in blackout they believed it might be transporting troops or war supplies. "He justified his action ... by the fact that the Zamzam was traveling completely blacked out, not even showing navigation lights, and by the fact that its outlines were identical with those of certain troop transports used by the British. ... He expressed deep personal regret over the entire tragedy."[117]

Indeed, the Germans had a public relations nightmare on their hands. The passengers were made up of mostly missionaries. One hundred forty-two of those

---

[117] V. Eugene Johnson, a survivor whose account appears in Swanson, S. Hjalmar, ed.; *Zamzam: The Story of a Strange Missionary Odyssey*; Minneapolis: The Board of Foreign Missions of the Augustana Synod, 1941; 63-64.

passengers were American and those were the days when Germany was making every overture in an attempt to keep the United States from entering the war.

German crew boarded and set three time bombs to complete the sinking of the *Zamzam*. The next day the rescued passengers were transferred to a German freighter named the *Dresden*. This boat turned into a true prison ship. Some of the crew of the *Dresden* were actually overheard calling the survivors "prisoners." Men were held crammed in the hold while women and children crowded into available cabins and lounges. Armed guards were everywhere. Food and even water was scarce. It turned out they would be on the *Dresden* for 33 days, mostly going in circles in the Atlantic, while the German command attempted to decide what to do.

The captain of the *Dresden*, who had seemed harsh in his first contact with the survivors, soon showed himself more hospitable. His name was Jaeger and he had himself been a prisoner of war for four years during World War I. He seemed to be doing what he could for the comfort of his new passengers, but his ship was not designed or equipped for that many people.

Many of the missionaries had saved their Bibles. For the next month, they read them a lot individually and in small groups. They were more than calm during their detention and there was no record of incident at all.

No one in the outside world was notified of the survival of the passengers and crew or even of the fact the *Zamzam* had been sunk. It appears to have been an intentional news blackout by the German command. Families and friends back home knew only the ship was missing.

Carlyle sent a ship-to-shore letter to his sister, Annie Kate (whom family called "Red"): "Landed Lagos safely April sixteenth stop Hope Rosa doing well." Later he wrote her about his work in Africa after his arrival: "Well, I have been here two weeks, nearly. I went up to our Convention and saw most of our missionary group and they were of the opinion I ought to spend a short while here helping Bro. Patterson[118] with his work. He is the man whose heart went bad some time ago and the Board asked me, as you will recall, to come and help out in a pinch."[119]

---

[118] Alonzo Scott Patterson.
[119] J. C. Powell at Lagos to Annie Kate Powell, April 27, 1941.

"Dear Daughter, Well, I have not heard a word from Mother since I left N. Y. I had an indirect message saying she had been delayed at Baltimore about two or three weeks. ... I understand the upcoast waiting list is pretty long - it may be July or August before she and the others get a chance to come. All we can do is wait and pray she will be kept safe."[120]

"Dear Daughter, I do not know what you may have heard but have not gotten any message from Mother yet. I suspect she is in Cape Town. Chances to come from there here are very limited. I keep thinking I will get a cable or letter or some news but things do not pan out with the news. She is with a good party and we will hear from them sometime. Whenever she gets here I will let you know as soon as I can."[121]

The very fact the *Dresden* could make circles in the Atlantic for so long without coming under Allied fire must surely have been an act of Providence. Finally the ship made its way through waters known to be under British blockade to the coast of German-occupied France. American passengers were disembarked at St. Jean de

---

[120] J. C. Powell at Lagos to Mary Hester Powell, May 5, 1941.
[121] J. C. Powell at Lagos to Mary Hester Powell, May 12, 1941.

Luz. Those of other nationalities were taken to Bordeaux. Eventually non-American men were placed in internment camps. Everyone else would be repatriated.

May 19 was the date of the arrival of the *Dresden* in France. It was also the day the first public information was released about the *Zamzam*. The first news announced only that the ship had been lost, presumed sunk and with very little hope at this late date anyone had survived. Back in the States, the Rocky Mount, N. C. newspaper headlined, "Mrs. Rosa Powell, Baptist Missionary, 6 Tobacco Men From Wilson Are Missing." Fortunately, the very next day the German government released news that all passengers and crew except one were alive and safe.

American passengers were detained at Biarritz, France for two more weeks while documents were secured. Then they were transported to the border with Spain and left by their German captors. It took another several weeks for them to be moved first to Portugal and then transported back to the States.

In France they were assisted by the American Red Cross and the American Friends Service Committee. Survivors would write of the actual starvation they observed among the occupied French people. It seemed to them, despite their condition, they fared much better than the French natives under occupation.

"One midnight we were high in the Pyrenees Mountains, when one of the cars of the train commenced to burn. Out into the rainy night we poured... to wait for another car. A journey that would take eight hours by a good train, took us thirty-two hours."[122]

As soon as news was released about the safety of the passengers, the Foreign Mission Board wired Carlyle and Mary Hester. On May 22, Mary Hester sent Maddry at the Foreign Mission Board a hand-written note thanking him for the wire and wondering if Rosa would go on to Africa or come back to the United States. For several weeks, that tiny little family of three were on three different continents.

On May 24, a secretary from the Foreign Mission Board wrote Mary Hester with an update that the missionaries were at Biarritz, France, almost to the Spanish border. "I know that all of this is upsetting to you especially at exam time. When I talked to Miss Baker the other night, she said that you were taking it all in a very sensible way, and I am glad that you can do this."

---

[122] Oiness, 32.

On June 1 the *Zamzam* survivors entered Portugal and eventually arrived in Lisbon. On June 3, Rosa telegraphed Mary Hester, "Well happy love to members of families friends thank God." She sat down at the Hotel Nunes Sintra on June 9 to write Mary Hester and the family: "We came to this place one week ago today. It has been good to be here, though Miss Elam has been in bed all the time since we arrived. She is up this A.M. and I hope will be able to stay up.

"We hope, however, to be leaving soon. Twenty-six unattached ladies will be the first group to go by boat. Some have gone, and others will go by plane. Five or six men from Wilson will perhaps leave by plane today or the middle of the week.

"Don't any of you worry about us any further. The Lord has led, delivered, comforted, strengthened and sustained in a marvelous way. Our essential needs have been met. The Lord willing, we hope to see you soon. Love to everyone."

The missionaries were still wondering if they would be allowed to proceed directly to Africa from there. "...a cable from the State Department in Washington, D. C., ordered American citizens... to return to America. That was a definite order. We had no choice in the matter."[123] The State Department explained they would not be allowed to travel directly to Africa because the routes the ships would take once more took them through a war zone.

The first group of 26 women survivors of the *Zamzam* returned to the United States aboard the Portuguese liner *Mouzinho*. It left on June 6 and arrived in New York on June 21. Other ships only days later would bring the remainder of the U.S. citizens home. Along with them came large numbers of Jewish refugees from Hitler's Europe. Rosa telegraphed Mary Hester at 5:45 PM "Arrived New York be North Carolina Monday night."

Three Southern Baptist missionaries, Rosa, Elma Elam and Isabella Moore, returned to the States. They would receive individual letters from Charles Maddry of the Foreign Mission Board: "I am writing this note to extend to you the joyous and cordial welcome of the Secretary and the Foreign Mission Board as you land in America. We suffered much anxiety and sorrow for several days thinking that you were all lost. It was a happy day when word came that you were safe.

"We welcome you back home and hope you will come by way of Richmond if it is

---

[123] Oiness, 34.

convenient. We are anxious to see you, and you will receive a rousing welcome throughout the South."[124]

Mary Hester had gone on to summer work at Mars Hill College (now University). She wrote her aunt, Naomi Chambers, that friends had come: "They corroborated Daddy's statement that he'd been down in Lagos helping Mr. A. Scott Patterson get his work done. They said they'd teased Daddy, not thinking he was seriously worried over Mother's not writing and told him that if he didn't stop worrying, Mother would not know him when she arrived. 'Well, she'll get about a thousand kisses from a strange man, then,' was his only reply. ... Mother's letter, written from Portugal, said that they were well, that their essential needs had been taken care of and that they hoped to be home soon."[125]

Missionary friend Hattie Gardner wrote Mary Hester of her Dad's strength: "It has been so hard for Mr. Powell but he has been so brave thru it all, altho I felt his heart was crushed. He has been an inspiration to me, to see how calm he has kept himself."[126]

---

[124] Charles Maddry to missionary survivors, June 17, 1941.
[125] Mary Hester Powell to Naomi Chambers, June 21, 1941.
[126] Hattie Gardner to Mary Hester Powell, June 9, 1941.

Finally, Rosa returned to Nigeria, landing in Monrovia, Liberia August 11 and in Lagos on September 6, 1941. In reporting expenses for the trip, Carlyle offered an aside which revealed his anguish during the summer: "Well I hope I never have an experience of this kind to face again. I was sure the whole crowd was in the bottom of the ocean. Death will not be more real than the sinking of the *Zamzam* was to me. For nearly four weeks I had been awaiting news that I had given up hope of receiving."[127]

But the mission work had gone on while the fate of the *Zamzamers* was unknown. In the same letter, Carlyle reported he'd baptized 71 since his return to Nigeria.

Uncertainty about Rosa had, however, taken its toll. Carlyle had lost 42 pounds.

"I heard one of our missionaries speak about seven miracles in connection with the *Zamzam* journey. These were some of them: That although fifty-five shots were fired at the *Zamzam*..., only nine reached their mark.... That although nine shells struck the *Zamzam*, no one aboard was killed. ... none of the missionaries were wounded. ... That although so many were cast into the open sea, among them

---

[127] J. C. Powell to Miss Newton at the Foreign Mission Board, September 15, 1941.

several small children, no one was drowned."
128

Surviving the shelling, the rescue, the crossing of Europe and years back in the United States is a little 3 X 5 memo book with only 18 pages total in it. It had been given as an advertising piece by Virginia-Carolina Fertilizers. Rosa carried it with her through the whole ordeal. The early pages carry notes from conversations including home remedies to be tried on some of her children. There is a list of passengers and some addresses, also handwritten. Then there are notes of the shelling, the transfer to the German raider and finally phrases in Portuguese for when they reached that country.

For decades survivors of the *Zamzam* met every few years for reunions. The reunions ended in 2016 when a dozen *Zamzamers* met at Lindsborg, Kansas. At this writing the website zamzamship.net is still active.

---

[128] Swanson, S. Hjalmar, ed.; *Zamzam: The Story of a Strange Missionary Odyssey*; Minneapolis: The Board of Foreign Missions of the Augustana Synod, 1941, 30.

**J.C. Powell baptizes in the river**

## Chapter 11
## Practical Guidance

*Long before I discovered book-length manuscripts from the pen of "Sky" Powell I was introduced to his writing by pamphlets he'd written and self-published. These were his efforts to further the spiritual growth of converts who knew almost nothing about their new Christian faith.*

### Practical Building Techniques

In developing Nigeria in the 1920s, constructing a building for church or school presented unique challenges. Limited building materials and even more limited skills meant the station missionary might be called upon to provide leadership never honed in any seminary classroom.

J. C. Powell turned out to be uniquely suited for these building projects. Though himself no contractor or engineer, Carlyle had the hands-on, problem-solving of a rural farm boy and the physical strength and agility of an athlete. He learned how to adapt the indigenous skills at building their mud-walled, thatched-roof houses. He built on the experience of other station missionaries before him. He introduced simple tools like the plumb line and designed other tools and techniques enabling the construction of even sizable buildings rapidly and with little cost.

In the 1920s and, to a lesser extent, in succeeding decades "Sky" Powell led the construction of scores of buildings. Some had mud walls and thatched roofs. Those would not survive more than a hand-full of years. Still, they were inexpensive enough to enable them to proliferate even in the bush and even in hard economic times. They were large enough to bring together a crowd of children to learn reading and Bible and adults to hear national preachers tell of Jesus. Those simple buildings were durable enough to become fixtures of faith in their villages and towns. They enabled local congregations to be built up so they, themselves, could construct their next generation's schools and churches.

Many other buildings constructed by "Sky" Powell and his teams of national builders were large and substantial buildings which withstood decades of use. Those had wood framing and metal roofs. Concrete block walls were needed in those buildings, since wood near the ground would immediately be eaten away by white ants.

## Nigerian Discipleship

Given the opportunity, J. C. Powell preached evangelistically and hard. Much of the time an interpreter accompanied him. National pastors and lay preachers also evangelized. But after people responded and publically acknowledged Jesus Christ, much discipling was still required.

Yoruba indigenous religions focused on actions, practices and physical representations (*orishas*) of their faith. When people responded to the Good News about Jesus, they usually assumed what was required of them was church attendance and outward worship. It fell the responsibility of the missionary to guide their discipling to a point they would understand and take seriously their spiritual lives. It was the missionary who helped bring them to the place of worshiping Christ alone at the expense of throwing away their idols. It was the missionary who guided them to reject their polygamist heritage and embrace biblical morality in many ways so different from what they had known.

Discipleship was a major challenge in firmly establishing national Nigerian churches. "After a stirring invitation, most everyone in the crowd might raise their hand to accept Christ and join the church with no intention of leaving off their idols. Sometimes it was necessary to put them on probation for as much as twelve to fifteen months."[129]

Only at the end of a lengthy discipleship process would Powell and other missionaries approve baptism of those new converts. And they baptized them by the hundreds.

As Nigerian Christian leadership emerged in strength, much of the discipling also passed to their responsibility. The Powells and other missionaries found themselves more and more in the roles of advisors to these uniquely called, gifted, qualified and educated Nigerian pastors and teachers.

**Mission Meetings**

Missionaries on every field are usually scattered and it is important for them to meet occasionally to keep each other informed of what is happening and to share personally and pray for one another. In the early years of the twentieth century, there were generally only a handful of missionaries in the whole country of Nigeria. It did not remain that way. Nigeria, the second mission theater for Southern Baptists, emerged as one of the largest in terms of personnel, programs and facilities.

---

[129] Powell, *Impressions*, 91.

Mary Hester Powell wrote to her Powell aunts about a Mission meeting at Ogbomoso. One hundred sixty-six had attended. There were ten "catering households" who provided food for all the people coming from far and wide. Sixteen people had been in her house for a week. She'd been to Oyo the weekend before to see her parents. "Mother and Daddy were trying to wind up one session of language school and get ready for another."[130]

In 1961, a letter was written on stationery of the "American Baptist Mission, Baptist Building, Ibadan. But the letter was written from Ogbomoso and reported the mission meeting where 166 missionaries and their 131 children had assembled. It was an update to emeritus missionaries of the actions of the mission and the movement and news among the missionaries. A personal note to the Powells reported, "Powell House won the cup at Sports Day this year."

## A Nigerian Convention

Organization of Baptist churches and work in Nigeria began as early as 1882 in Lagos in an "associational theological institute"

---

[130] Mary Hester Powell to her Powell aunts, September 5, 1954.

162

and the revival it sparked. The mission adopted a constitution for the first time in 1910 and provided for a yearly "native workers' conference." In 1914 the Yoruba Baptist Association was organized and included independent Baptist churches as well as those associated with the Foreign Mission Board of the Southern Baptist Convention. It shortly changed its name to the Nigerian Baptist Convention.

After half-a-century in Nigeria, the Southern Baptist Mission could report in 1900 only six churches, six outstations and 385 members. In 1914, when the Yoruba Association formed, there were 31 churches and 2880 members. More than half of those came from the independent churches. By 1950, reflecting the time of the Powells and their colleagues careers, there were 350 churches with 24,000 members and with 200 Nigerian pastors assisted by a hundred Foreign Mission Board missionaries. It had also been a period that saw the rise of Baptist hospitals, seminary and training schools and institutions of almost every kind.[131]

Of the need for Christian leadership with connectedness to the indigenous people,

[131] Statistics from Baker James Cauthen. *Advance: A History of Southern Baptist Foreign Missions*. Broadman, 1970. 146-152.

Carlyle wrote: "My opinion is any man you might pick for the job [of General Secretary] ought to spend ten to twelve years on the field before he takes over the work. You cannot select a man for that job, he has to grow to it. ... It is the most important job we have on the field. It will take a vast larger knowledge of the people than it will of the language."[132]

Education for pastors received high priority - more as the years went by. "We tried to make educational levels a basis for leaders' financial support. Situations differed. Men who could read and teach only in Yoruba generally received five to seven dollars a month in stipend in the early years we were there."[133]

As important as education was, however, practical understanding of congregational dynamics was equally significant. "I discovered the pastors who were most successful were the ones who had learned how to manage the small groups in his church and put them to work. Many of the small groups had pledges they would make and keep within their group."[134]

---

[132] J. C. Powell to Charles Maddry, August 18, 1935.

[133] Powell, *Impressions*, 92.

[134] Ibid., 88.

## Islam and Indigenous Religion

Even though the greatest influence of Christian missionaries by far was in the Southwestern Region of Nigeria, even there roughly one-third of the population was Muslim. They exerted tremendous pressure on Christian churches, missions and individual believers in that region.

"The Mohamedans can get any place they want to put up a mask [sic]. But sometimes it can take us years to get a place for a church. Tell the trustees not to close their eyes to facts. Mohamid [sic] is not dead."[135]

To the North, Muslims held an overwhelming majority. For a long time no Baptist missionaries ventured into that region, the Mission preferring to focus on the more receptive Southwest. Not until 1949 was the first missionary residence constructed in Kaduna, making it the first Southern Baptist mission station in the Muslim North.

Indigenous population of Nigeria during most of the Powells' service there could be equally divided into three religious groups. In addition to Christianity and Islam, native religion still held considerable influence. Often the people would adopt Christianity without

---

[135] J. C. Powell to T. Bronson Ray, July 8, 1921.

thoroughly rejecting their idols or the magic that surrounded them.

With considerable satisfaction, Rosa wrote Mary Hester about the son of a king who remained absolutely committed to his new Christian faith: "Last week the king in this town died. His eldest son, just 18 years, refused to allow his father to be buried according to native custom. He had a proper coffin made for him. And later he refused to become his father's successor as king because... he knew the people would force him to worship idols as is the custom with most rulers in this country." She went on to say he had applied to the Baptist College and Seminary.[136]

## African Culture

First Baptist Church Lagos had been rocked by division as early as 1888 when most of its members withdrew to form Native Baptist Church (later Ebenezer Baptist Church) and was counted the first culturally African church. Even at that early date there emerged contrast and even conflict between missionary sponsored churches and separate African culture churches

---

[136] Rosa Powell from Shaki to Mary Hester Powell, December 18, 1934.

No issue was more culturally charged than polygamy. Polygamy was generally rejected by missionaries of all Christian denominations. "Many African church leaders believed the missionaries' perspective on monogamy was influenced by their culture and was therefore not to be imposed on Africans."[137]

In the early twentieth century, the Nigerian Baptist churches led by national pastors and those still drawing from American missionaries cooperated and were generally content in the same convention. That was at least partially because the Foreign Mission Board and the Southern Baptist Convention wanted Nigerian Baptist churches to develop into autonomy. As early as 1947 ownership of the Baptist schools passed to the Nigerian Baptist Convention.

As the time for Nigerian independence approached, the people and churches of the Nigerian Baptist Convention sought ever more native leadership and decision-making. Distinctives of Nigerian culture were also not only tolerated but embraced. Mary Hester Powell used (maybe coined) the word "Nigerianization" to describe the movement. Generally throughout the Mission and the

---

[137] Ayodeji Abodunde. *A Heritage of Faith: A History of Christianity in Nigeria*; 2017. 263.

Board it was called more broadly "indigenization." That intentional effort to move Foreign Mission Board churches, programs and institutions to indigenous leadership and control as quickly as possible represented Board policy not only with regards to the Nigerian mission, but with mission work globally.

## Polygamy

As late as 1939 polygamy remained a major contention. Carlyle remained adamant in his opposition as did most missionaries. Details emerged of a treasurer in one church who was practicing polygamy and had also been caught loaning out church money for his own gain. Carlyle had the church rolls purged of all polygamists. The treasurer had many friends and supporters. He let it be known to people in the church who opposed him if they came into the marketplace they would get a thrashing. Carlyle told the people to go about their business, be gentle, and accept any abuse because their Lord was abused as well.[138]

Despite British efforts at eradicating polygamy, it continued to be widely practiced the whole time of the Powells' appointment. Because polygamy was understood by almost

---

[138] J. C. Powell to Charles Maddry, March 30, 1939.

all of the missionaries as in direct opposition to biblical command and expectation, missionaries, including J. C. Powell, opposed it vigorously in the churches. Even with that opposition, there was resistance from polygamist leaders of the churches, some national pastors and even the occasional missionary. When the national church movement began in earnest in Nigeria, tolerance of polygamy as a distinctive Nigerian cultural trait was largely built into practice. It became a contention between locally-led churches and those still accepting guidance from Western missionaries.

In March 1939, Carlyle said in a letter he had opposed the polygamists for 20 years and he thought it would take four to eight more years to settle the issue. A pastor had taken a second wife. Powell required him to resign and turn in his ordination papers. "I never hunt with my gun half cocked," Carlyle wrote of his firm action.

Apparently the same issue was still festering at the end of the year. "...he thinks Pastor Imosun is partly responsible for his losing his ordination. ...so he has been going to Aha, a city ten miles from here, from one to six times a week hiring a witch doctor to make medicine to run Pastor Imosun out of town. Of

course, the Juju man ... gets money for the job."
[139]

Indeed, the struggle continued. It was posed, as it had been 20 years before, as a cultural conflict. When Powell brought the matter to a Nigerian Baptist Convention he was met with the retort, "None of your abuse for our customs."[140] A year later he reported financial stress in some churches because polygamists had cut off giving in an effort to starve out anti-polygamist pastors.[141]

Even after Carlyle and Rosa retired, the polygamy issue continued to surface in the Nigerian Baptist Convention: "On May 1st, the Nigerian Baptist Convention met in Ogbomosho for its forty-third session. There were over eleven hundred delegates registered.... One of the sessions which I'm sure will be remembered for a long time was the one in which the question of polygamy was discussed. For many years it has been one of our serious problems. The policy in the past has been to baptize only the first wife of a polygamist. This year the convention ruled that neither a polygamist nor any of his wives can be baptized and become a church member.

[139] J. C. Powell at Shaki to Mary Hester Powell, December 19, 1939.
[140] J. C. Powell to Charles Maddry, June 7, 1939.
[141] J. C. Powell to Charles to Maddry, February 26, 1940.

When the question was called for there were only four who voted against it."[142]

## Divorce

What about divorce? In talking about the importance of culture, he recounted a man who had inherited a wife. She "quit" him and married another man and he subsequently remarried. "Now knowing the mental background of these people, is it wise to advise the church to select another or is it wise to advise giving him a chance to win out under the peculiar circumstances? Twelve years ago I would have said the last word and that would have been "get, and look another job," but I know native mind too well to be that hasty now. I may let him go and more than likely will, but I aim to get all the evidence possible first."[143]

## A System of Education

From the earliest days of Southern Baptist work in Nigeria a system developed in providing education. A school began when a missionary simply gathered a group of

---

[142] Margaret and Henry Martin to J. C. and Rosa Powell, June 17, 1957.
[143] J. C. Powell to Charles Maddry, August 18, 1935.

children around and began to teach them to read. Initially there might be little interest on the part of the kids and parents. As soon as parents did begin to appreciate education for their children they were asked to help provide that education by paying a small tuition or bringing in-kind donations.

Some children who lived a distance from the school became boarding students. They did chores including working in a garden to produce food consumed by them and their fellow students and the teacher.

Participation by parents and children in providing their education made the whole experience more valuable to them and helped insure their dedicated work in learning as well. Their support also enabled more and larger schools to be built and teachers to be employed. In the long run, a sense of autonomy and self-sufficiency emerged among the parents and students which helped foster indigenous leadership and ownership of churches and schools and ultimately contributed to successful emergence of Nigerian independence.

Bringing in students from everywhere in a developing country meant the necessity of teaching hygiene. Teachers and administrators also had to go to extreme measures to guard against disease and insects. Rosa wrote once about the added job of "boiling off" the clothes of new students who came to her school.

When Rosa talked about her teaching, she sounded much like any American teacher: "I like teaching when I have time to do it properly and I do not have discipline problems."[144]

A teacher was found to be drinking their local, low-alcohol beer. Carlyle insisted he would put him out as a teacher even though he had no replacement and might have to close the school. He would not allow him to remain and be a bad influence on the children.[145]

## Practical Demands Back Home

Hester Hocutt's health continued to decline. Early in 1944 a series of letters from back home described her ill health. Mary Hester was so attached to her grandmother Hocutt, she called her "Mama," usually calling Rosa "Mother". Writing January 17 of that year, Mary Hester said "Mama" had almost died several times and the doctors had said her body was simply wearing out. She'd been in the Wilmington hospital, had several

---

[144] Rosa Powell to her mother, June 22, 1947.
[145] J. C. Powell to Charles Maddry, March 30, 1939.

transfusions, and suffered from uremic poisoning.

In February a letter came from a close family friend: "Mother Hocutt seems somewhat improved, but all medical science fails to give hope of a real recovery from her heart condition." He went on to describe at length her thin heart walls and poor heart function which made her tired all the time. Still, she wanted to work in her garden. "Mary Hester told her that she would plant her some okra in a shoebox and let her dig with a spoon all she desires. Can't you see the real Mary Hester in that statement."[146]

That winter was also a time of upheaval in Mary Hester's life. A gentleman friend had become more and more important to her. They were close enough he attended family functions with her. Family and friends had wondered aloud to her if they were destined to marry. Although she continued to insist they were nowhere near that step, clearly they had a special relationship. The war had taken him away from her. The winter of 1943-44 witnessed the cooling of her lieutenant's ardor. "Mother, you asked if we were getting married. Heavens, No! I'm further from it than I've ever

---

[146] Lewis Harper Dawson to Carlyle and Rosa, February 7, 1944. Dawson had met Mary Hester at Ridgecrest Camp and considered her an adopted sister.

been since I've known the young Lt. ... I haven't heard from him since the week before Christmas - except for his Christmas present. ... Saturday I mailed the letter of resignation. It was really more on the order of 'please tell me where I stand'. ... asked if there were anyone else in whom he was interested.... At least I've found out you don't die over these things."[147] In fact, the relationship was over.

---

[147] Mary Hester Powell to her parents, January 17, 1944.

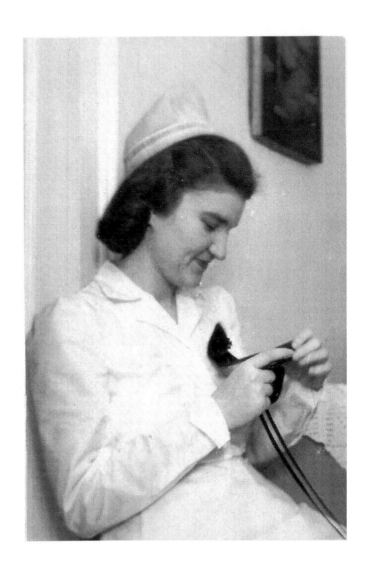

**Mary Hester Powell**

## Chapter 12
## Missionary Nurse

*On February 15, 2018 we gathered in Mary Hester Powell's room at her life-care facility in Greenville, North Carolina. There was an interviewer from the International Mission Board of the Southern Baptist Convention, a video team from Clinton, North Carolina along with Kathryn Hamrick (Mary Hester's cousin), my wife and me. The IMB was doing a two-hour interview with Mary Hester to serve as an oral history of her recollections.*

Mary Hester Powell graduated from Meredith College in the class of 1942, about the time she turned 20 years of age. The school's annual, *Oak Leaves*, lists beside her senior picture her accomplishments and involvements while at the college: choir, hockey, *Twig* staff, glee club, student legislative assembly, granddaughters' club, sociology club, class treasurer.

After her graduation, Mary Hester followed her mother into teaching. For two years she taught Social Science at Southwood High School in Kinston, North Carolina.

In the summer of 1943 she served as secretary in the social workers' office at Kennedy Home in Kinston. Kennedy Home was then and is now a major campus of Baptist Children's Homes in North Carolina.

## Called to Nursing, Called to Nigeria

Mary Hester wrote to Charles Maddry at the Foreign Mission Board on March 6, 1944 about her frustration with teaching. "This makes my second year here in Kinston. School teaching has given me three gray hairs and a wisdom tooth, plus a new supply of anecdotes. That being the case, don't you think it advisable for me to make a change?" Maddry wrote back on March 8: "I really think that you have taught long enough, and it is about time now for you to go on to the Training School in Louisville, marry a fine young pastor or missionary prospect for Africa and thus settle the whole matter."

Frustrated with teaching, Mary Hester returned to Warsaw and took a job as a receptionist in a doctor's office (1944-1945). She had apparently always considered nursing an alternative career and the experience in the doctor's office confirmed her vocational choice. She entered the Johns Hopkins University School of Nursing, graduating in 1948.

To help get her through nursing school, she joined the Cadet Nurse Corp. She mentioned to the Foreign Mission Board that technically she could be drafted into military service at any time due to that commitment. In 1948 she became an office nurse in Warsaw.

Her correspondence with her parents and with contacts at the Foreign Mission Board continued. She was uncertain about missions. Like her mother before her, Mary Hester was worried about leaving behind her Hocutt and Powell families. She wrote in her application to the Foreign Mission Board, "In the event one of the aunts with whom I have made my home should become totally incapacitated, I should consider resigning - if there seemed to be no other satisfactory solution to the problem."

Receiving guidance from Richmond, Mary Hester went to Nigeria first as a contract worker. As that contract came to an end, she had the appointment "regularized." The Board was happy to have another much-needed nurse on the field.

When Mary Hester was being considered as a contract worker for Nigeria - her first venture into mission service - her Dad was of mixed feelings: "The whole thing has come like a cloud burst on me. I hardly know what to think. All I know is I want her to be where God wants her to be. I have refrained and have not talked with her about it for I did not want my influence as father to have any bearing on her life movements."[148]

Sadler would write to Rosa about Mary Hester on March 21, 1949 that she had made a "very favorable impression" on the Appointment Committee at the Foreign Mission Board. "She seems to have her feet firmly planted on a solid foundation."

Mary Hester would spend most of her mission career in Ogbomoso and Eku working in the hospitals there and ultimately teaching and administering in the schools of nursing.

## Urgent Need For Nurses

Mary Hester Powell entered missions when Southern Baptists were at perhaps their most effective time in Nigeria. In 1950 the Nigerian Baptist Convention celebrated the one hundredth anniversary of Baptist work in the province. George W. Sadler had led the college and seminary at Ogbomoso and later was elected Secretary for Africa, Europe and the Near East. His report in 1950 revealed that there were "'119 missionaries under appointment, four teacher-training institutions, four medical centers with doctors, three medical centers with nurses in charge, five

---

[148] J. C. Powell to George W. Sadler, March 2, 1949.

secondary schools, 350 day (grammar) schools, one seminary, one Bible school. Baptisms reported during the last convention year totaled 2,044."[149]

"Diseases of all kinds ran rampant in the country. Those diseases attacking the respiratory system were frequently fatal because Yoruba did not have sufficient clothing or bedding and did not understand how to treat a patient with pneumonia or tuberculosis. The influenza pandemic took a heavy toll on the country with an estimated 15 to 40 percent of the population succumbing."[150]

Quite rapidly Southern Baptist medical missions drew public and governmental attention. Natives would travel for miles to bring sick family members to be treated in Baptist dispensaries and hospitals. Chiefs would send representatives and sometimes gifts in efforts to draw Baptist medical presence to their villages. The result was constant overcrowding in the hospitals and constant shortages of nurses. Mary Hester wrote once there were 74 patients in a 56-bed

---

[149] Estep, William R. *Whole Gospel Whole World: The Foreign Mission Board of the Southern Baptist Convention 1845-1995.* Nashville: Broadman & Holman, 1994. 270.
[150] Powell, *Impressions*, 59.

hospital and objected that doctors were too ready to admit patients.[151]

"The Yoruba commonly bathed and dipped drinking water from the same springs. Dysentery was frequent along with various varieties of intestinal worms including tape, round and hook. Sometimes a single patient would be found with all three varieties of intestinal worms."[152]

"The most terrifying disease of all was probably leprosy. The Yoruba people were so afraid of leprosy that lepers were regularly driven out into the bush. Early in our tenure, only three small residences offered accommodation to lepers. The general rule was to drive them to the bush to avoid the spread of the disease."[153]

A leper colony called "Camp of Hope" had been established just outside Ogbomoso and Baptist missionaries assisted with the work there with great appreciation from the government. Mary Hester wrote of visiting there on several occasions. Most notably was a letter reporting her attendance at a discharge service for 36 patients including the

---

[151] March 31, 1957.
[152] Powell, *Impressions,* 61.
[153] Ibid., 62.

headmaster who had been a patient for 13 years.[154]

If leprosy was the most terrifying disease, malaria was perhaps the most common. Nigerians developed some resistance to the disease. Missionaries took daily doses of quinine. Even so, recurrences of malaria were so common they were almost a fact of life. Mary Hester would note mater-of-factly, "I'd write a typed letter, but Emma's had malaria and I don't want to disturb her."[155]

In 1949, Mary Hester was working in Ogbomoso in the OB unit at Frances Jones Memorial Home. It was a facility built to care for missionaries. She wrote to her aunt and uncle that she felt badly about not being at the main hospital since they were so understaffed. Nevertheless, there were three new Moms at the center and another baby due.[156]

In another letter, she remarked she had to close as the lights were about to go out at the mission compound. Electricity was on at the Ogbomoso mission complex only from 6:30 until 11:00 each evening.[157]

---

[154] Mary Hester Powell to the Chambers and Powells, January 15, 1957.
[155] March 17, 1957.
[156] Mary Hester Powell to Naomi and David Chambers, September 3, 1949.
[157] November 2, 1949.

## A Family of Missionaries

Mary Hester would serve as a missionary nurse in Nigeria for 13 years. While on her first furlough, she worked in Winston-Salem at Baptist Hospital from October 1952 until April 1953.

It was during that 1952-1953 furlough that Mary Hester received a visit from a well-dressed, blonde man who identified himself as a member of some U.S. information service. He wanted to talk to her and her parents. "With that, he proceeded to ask detailed questions about communistic activities in Nigeria; the state of the roads, airports, educational and medical facilities, the building of hydroelectric projects, water supplies, and so on...." She had been evasive with the agent and later wrote Theron Rankin at the Foreign Mission Board asking if there was any policy on talking with government agents.

Rankin replied the man was probably from the CIA and she could feel free to give them information that would have been general information available to the public. "We must keep clear the fact that we are in no way serving as agents of our government. At the same time, I can see no reason why we should refrain from giving to government representatives any information that we would give to other people in general."[158]

Mary Hester had found herself caught between two political movements. In Nigeria there was a growing cry for independence and some occasional experimentation with communist philosophy. In the United States there was the urgent searching out of anything communist in the age of McCarthy.

It would not be the last time she reflected on communist influence in Nigeria. She would write on March 23, 1958 "We had a lightning strike of P. T. [public transit] employees (two days) this last week. *Daily Times* was most emphatic in its disgust with communist methods.... Looks as if the communists have quite a strong hold already - that was probably just the beginning."

There was fun to be had in Nigeria. For Carlyle, it was often hunting and shooting. For Rosa it was gardening. Mary Hester did her share of traveling and shopping. She wrote to her Powell family that she and her parents had

---

[158] M. Theron Rankin to Mary Hester Powell, September 8, 1952.

taken "local leave" and had an all-day picnic at a park some 50 miles away.[159]

Carlyle's stunts and antics mixed with recreation. Onboard the *M.V. Apapa* of the Elder Dempster line returning from furlough in 1953, Mary Hester wrote back to Warsaw, "Daddy entered the quoits contest (something like horseshoes - but you throw rope rings onto a court of concentric circles....)" On the same voyage, there was a carnival night where evening clothes was the attire. Instead, Carlyle (with their help, it appears) dressed in women's clothes. "He waltzed across the deck once with one of the gentlemen and brought the house down!"[160]

In yet another letter (date unclear), Mary Hester laughed about Daddy being in the opening scene of a Foreign Mission Board film on Nigeria missions. "They told me he kept the acting going." She noted that words and music would be added to the film later so his own comments would not be audible. "I dare say his ad-libbing wouldn't fit the movie anyway."

---

[159] February 16, 1955.
[160] July 11, 1953.

## Ogbomoso

In 1954 Mary Hester began working at the baby building and the sick missionary house in Ogbomoso. In a circular letter of March 28, 1954, she described the constitution of a church at the seminary chapel in Ogbomoso: "Today a church was organized. It was a dignified and thought-provoking service in the Seminary Chapel. Begun several years ago as a morning service in which four interpreters were used, it has grown and increased in usefulness till time for formal organization has come....

"The student pastors at the Nigerian Baptist Theological Seminary are called upon to 'shepherd the flocks' in the villages within a radius of fifteen or more miles of Ogbomoso. Their wives with heavy family responsibilities do not travel out....

"Busy student nurses, with full schedules of classes and ward duty made up a large segment of the congregation on Sunday mornings, and were in the majority of those who became charter members of the church.

"Houseboys from the 'East' (eastern Nigeria, that is) are present in impressive numbers at the Sunday morning services usually.

"The M.K.'s (Missionary Kids), coming in from their own little Sunday School, and their missionary elders who are not called upon to be elsewhere, are at 'Eastern Antioch' in ever-increasing numbers these days."

As was often the case with most missionaries, Mary Hester was called upon to write to groups back home including children's classes who wanted information about what missionaries do. At the time of this letter to a church's Intermediate Department, Mary Hester was working at the Kersey Children's Home in Ogbomoso. "There are about 35 children at the Home. Most of them are under six years old. They have a little Nursery School to help them know how to wash their hands, how to brush their teeth with chewing sticks, how to play together, sharing their toys. There and in their Sunday School classes they hear the same Bible stories that you hear, and sing some of the same choruses and songs that you sing - all in a different language from yours, a language called *Yoruba*."[161]

Mary Hester brought together her teaching and nursing careers beginning September 28, 1956. That was when she began teaching at the nursing school connected with Ogbomoso Baptist Hospital. Nursing trainers

---

[161] October 7, 1955.

were called "Sister Tutors" in the British system. During her entire career in nursing and teaching, Mary Hester regularly shared her witness for Jesus Christ with patients and actively looked for opportunities to do so.

By mid-century, Nigeria was rapidly developing. That did not mean even basic necessities came easily. Mary Hester wrote to her aunt and uncle, David and Naomi Chambers, "... have had several storms lately.... We have more water than we'ver had in our tank; hope our commode doesn't keep running now, or we'll be low again. That reminds me, please send by airmail one rubber tank ball, No. 2650 (Rite Fit). Bill Williams fixed ours this a.m., and we'll need one."[162]

Facilities were also in need of major repair or replacing at Eku hospital. When Dr. and Mrs. Baker James Cauthen visited early in 1957, Mary Hester wrote home, "I think they were impressed with the need for 'water-bourne' sanitation in this about-to-tumble-down hospital.[163]

---

[162] October 13, 1957.
[163] March 10, 1957.

## On the Wards, In the Dispensaries

Overcrowding was a constant problem in the hospitals. Word was out of the effectiveness of the medical care and the prayer and support given in these facilities. Mary Hester's letters home often referenced the nurses hardly having room to move about and do their work. On one occasion she reported the pediatrics ward designed for twelve patients had twenty-eight and seven more had been placed in the women's ward. The patients were two and three to a bed. Added to that was the fact most patients, especially the children, were accompanied by family members or friends they called "attendants." Ostensibly there to help meet the needs of the patient, they usually were mostly impediments to the nurses.[164]

There were spiritual results from the daily medical duty of the hospitals. In a mass letter back home, Aletha Fuller at Mary Hester's hospital reported the case of an obstetrical patient who had already delivered eight dead babies but continued to wear *Juju* beads around her wrist for good luck. The Christian midwife urged her to cut off the *Juju* beads saying it had done nothing to bring her healthy babies. The patient said, "Bring blade" and announced she'd trust Jesus only from

---

[164] Mary Hester Powell letter of April 8, 1957.

then on. "Within five minutes this very woman delivered a fine, normal, beautiful, eight-pound baby."[165]

Outbreaks of illness could bury the medical staff in new cases: "There's really a small pox epidemic raging now. It's the worst one I've heard of since I've been in the country. They are even stopping travelers on the highway, asking to see a recent scar or, in our case, our certificates of vaccination. ... Hospital in Ibadan are closed to everything but small pox at the moment. Emma and Ruth Womack [166] vaccinated 308 people yesterday afternoon alone; and we've been doing them at that rate off and on for two weeks now!"[167]

## A Trip North

Nursing was not her only missionary activity. When she was not on the floors or teaching nursing, Mary Hester was traveling, usually accompanied by other women missionaries. They did a variety of work in support of Sunday School and Women's Missionary Union.

---

[165] Letter of March 3, 1957.
[166] Emma Mildred Watts (?) and Mary Ruth Womack.
[167] Mary Hester Powell to "folks,' February 5, 1957.

In a mimeographed letter back home in 1955, Mary Hester reported she was on a trip to Kaduna, the only place in Northern Nigeria with a Southern Baptist mission station. She was traveling with Bonnie Moore to do Sunday School work and a Sunday School conference.

In another letter, Mary Hester reflected upon the need for Christian mission work among the Muslims: "It is said of this section ... given ten years without a tremendous advance in Christian missionary activity, this territory will be closed to us forever by the rapidly on-running tide of Mohammedism." She went on to note their own mission had chosen not to expand north due to lack of personnel. She concluded, "Medical work is the key to Christianizing the Moslem world...!"

In a letter to her friends written from Eku Baptist Hospital, Mary Hester wrote, "The hospital affairs have settled down (for me at least) into a round of mornings on the wards, trying to observe all the students at once! ... Afternoons are spent in classes, or preparing for or grading papers... As usual, we need more nurses."

**J.C. Powell with J.W. Richardson**
**both Nigerian missionaries**
**ca 1958**

## Chapter 13
## Home Again

*Many missionaries retire and return home for years, even decades, of recounting their experiences for the benefit of churches, family and friends. For this family, the weakened health of Carlyle Powell soon narrowed their world mostly to Warsaw. People even today remember them as fixtures at the church and around the community.*

Rosa's teaching later in her career was at the Oyo Boys High School. She and Carlyle served as well in the Language and Orientation School in Oyo to help prepare incoming missionaries.

As early as June 6, 1946, George Sadler was mentioning in letters to Carlyle and Rosa of their possible need to retire due to Carlyle's health. Later that year,[168] Carlyle mentioned in a letter to Sadler that both he and Rosa were teaching in school that year. He was teaching Bible and she English Composition. Clearly he was not as much in the bush as in previous years. Even so, in the same year he wrote Sadler several times detailing the need of procuring roof metal for a middle school they were building.

---

[168] September 18.

The letters received by the Foreign Mission Board began to be more from Rosa than from Carlyle. "Carl is about to work himself sick. He has fever today. We hope it will pass. He has put every ounce of energy he had into the building...."

Carlyle's already declining health was exasperated by injury. He wrote to Sadler he had fallen four or five feet into a newly dug pit on a site. He had hurt his back and knee. A blood clot had arisen in the knee causing swelling and discoloration. At the time he was in the Frances Jones Home in Ogbomoso.[169]

Needs at home were becoming more incumbent as well: "We do not know when we shall go home, but my mother has been sick for so long that I feel the need of getting home to help take care of her."[170] They did make it home on furlough the beginning of May. On May 27, Sadler wrote Rosa with condolences on the passing of her mother.

During the 1952-53 furlough, Carlyle's health had so declined the family was concerned. His brother William, an attorney at Carolina Beach, wrote Sadler at the Foreign Mission Board of his and the family's concern. He asked his letter be kept confidential but

---

[169] J. C. Powell to George W. Sadler, January 15, 1951.
[170] Rosa Powell to George W. Sadler, January 18, 1948.

indicated Carlyle had all his teeth extracted and was so weak he couldn't walk a mile. He told Sadler the consensus of all the brothers and sisters was "if he is sent back, he will never return again alive."[171]

Sadler immediately replied to William he had also noticed Carlyle's decline when he had visited Richmond. He reported that while retirement age was 65, with a doctor's advice he could get his annuity at once. But he acknowledged he could not second-guess the doctors if they cleared Carlyle for service.[172]

Rosa wrote to Baker J. Cauthen: "It is most difficult to submit to the idea of retirement, but I realize that my husband is not physically fit to be on the field now. We thank God that he - my husband - has improved some. We hope that he can carry on with a reasonable amount of deputation work in behalf of Nigeria. ... We rejoice that Mary Hester was able to return to Nigeria, and pray that she may be a power for good during this and the coming years of service."[173]

In fact, the couple was able to return to the field for another tour in 1953. At the end of the year, Rosa wrote friends from her station in

---

[171] Letter of May 25, 1953.
[172] Letter of May 26, 1953.
[173] March 24, 1953.

Oyo. She talked about heartbreaking troubles on the field which sapped the energies of the missionaries. Then she recounted joys including 286 baptisms in four of their churches.

Rosa wrote to Sadler that the other missionaries at the station were of the opinion they should return home early because of Carlyle's health. She believed they should return home before Christmas.[174] They did, indeed, make the return to the States that year. Sadler wrote: "You have certainly poured yourself into that work, and we appreciate all you have accomplished both through your efforts and through the giving of your daughter. Certainly you have made an indelible impression upon many lives in that important part of the world."[175]

Carlyle commented to friends back at Warsaw Baptist Church the hardest thing he ever had to do was come home on retirement without Mary Hester.

As always, when they returned home they expected to both be kept busy speaking at churches on behalf of missions. Carlyle went through medical examinations upon return to

---

[174] Rosa Powell to George W. Sadler, February 2, 1955.
[175] George W. Sadler to J. C. and Rosa Powell, September 29, 1955.

the United States. It was Rosa who received a letter from Sadler's secretary at the Foreign Mission Board saying the doctor believed "that he might fill some speaking engagements but should not be expected to carry out any sustained efforts."[176]

Mary Hester wrote of her Dad's condition that he "had several rounds of what seemed to be malaria since he came home, but on the whole seems a bit better. His new teeth fit better and his new glasses 'see' better, and I think the high-powered vitamins have pepped him up a bit." She went on to say he should be able to accept a good number of speaking engagements.[177]

By mid-1957 Carlyle and Rosa had taught in five schools of mission as emeritus missionaries. For their work, the Foreign Mission Board sent a check for a total of $300 - $25 honorarium and $5 incidental fee for each of them for each school.[178]

The Baptist Foreign Mission Board minutes for November 8, 1956 carried the following recognition: "The Foreign Mission Board in regular monthly session records its

---

[176] January 6, 1956.
[177] Mary Hester Powell to George W. Sadler, April 2, 1956.
[178] Letter accompanying check from Foreign Mission Board, May 13, 1957.

thanks for the life and work of Julius Carlyle and Rosa Hocutt Powell whose service as active missionaries comes to a close on November 30, 1956. For thirty-seven years these missionaries have given themselves to the task of enlightening the peoples of Nigeria.

"We are grateful also for the contribution they have made in the person of their only child, Miss Mary Hester Powell, who follows in her parents' footsteps as a missionary to Nigeria."

With her parents back home and health seemingly returning to her Daddy, Mary Hester returned to her mission work. On January 10, 1957, she wrote to Sadler that she had recently arrived in Ibadan and was trying to "get my feet on the ground in the nursing school program". One of her cousins, Jeanette Scott, also came to serve in Nigeria as a contract worker. In 1958 she was at Ibadan at the Baptist Building there and Mary Hester had the opportunity to spend Christmas that year with her. Before long Mary Hester was back in Ogbomoso.

At the hospitals, mental as well as physical health issues were exposed. Mary Hester wrote home once about a senior in the nursing program who had attempted suicide by drinking cleaners. Sent to the government run University College Hospital, amazingly she had survived. A young man who was a patient had gotten into an argument with his father. He had run all over campus in the night shouting and finally jumped into a pit which had been dug for a new latrine. The next day, staff had to take the top off the latrine to get him out.[179]

Something else happened in 1958. Telephone service came to Ogbomosho. Mary Hester wrote triumphantly that there was a "red-front booth at the post office."[180]

She wrote of cultural-laden events such as the naming of a baby. It was a worship experience complete with hymns and scriptures. Then anyone who wanted could come forward to give the baby a name ... and the parents a gift. "One Yoruba name that he was given meant 'Born to Live' (which is most appropriate when one considers the enormous infant mortality rate out here)."[181]

She worried over a discipline problem in one of her letters: "We had a few discipline problems among some ... students at the nursing school last week - a couple of students

---

[179] October 26, 1958.
[180] February 7, 1958.
[181] Mary Hester Powell to David and Naomi Chambers, November 24, 1957.

refused to take a test of mine (said they hadn't had sufficient warning) and nearly got kicked out of the nursing school, because it's on the basis of that same attitude that they could refuse to carry out a doctor's order. ... That sort of thing could happen on either side of the pond however; so I don't feel that we have an individual problem there."[182]

There was a nursing shortage as there almost always was, not only in Nigeria but everywhere. Cornell Goerner, Secretary for Africa, Europe and the Near East, wrote Mary Hester on July 1, 1959 of the shortage, "It is our greatest single headache just now all over the world."

As Nigeria developed as a nation, some of the greatest changes were to the educational system. New requirements were constantly introduced to every level of education. For the village schools it meant their teachers had to have more certification. As a result, there began to be a shortage of qualified teachers. In the professional schools, there was heightened requirements for graduates. Several times Mary Hester wrote home about the difficulty in graduating students from the nursing schools. In 1957 she noted only three of sixteen students had passed their government exam on the first attempt. She then went into a lengthy

[182] February 9, 1958.

objection to British examiners who had no experience in Nigerian healthcare. She concluded the students might have to learn by rote the specific answers they knew the examiners wanted them to give.[183]

Failure in the governmental exams had a demoralizing effect upon the student nurses. Many left the program rather than try again. As a result, the nurse shortage in Nigeria was further exacerbated. "...several students in the Junior Class in the nursing school resigned ... leaving only one in that class...."[184]

While nursing and the medical needs of the people consumed much of her time, there was always the overarching spiritual needs of the people and the missionary families. On one occasion she'd gone to visit a discharged patient. A man of the family had brought out his Koran and began to insist Jesus was not the Son of God. She'd witnessed to the truth of the Gospel as best she could, but later wrote home, "We'll have to take the pastor who visits in the hospital a lot, who was once a moslem [sic] himself, to talk to him in Yoruba...."[185]

Back in Ogbomoso, the spiritual needs were ever more complex: "At the close of

---

[183] Letter of March 3.
[184] Mary Hester's letter of March 11, 1958.
[185] Letter of May 25, 1958.

Sunday School this morning I counted six languages (including English) that were spoken in the various classes. This particular church serves people from Eastern Nigeria where the many tribal groups each have a different language or dialect. Some of the congregation were hospital staff; some students in the seminary here, some Eastern school teachers in the town.... Ogbomoso is in the heart of Yoruba country; but these folk come to a worship service in English because it is a common language for them."[186]

Mary Hester was separated from her parents again, as she had been during her teen and college years. What was more, her Powell aunts were advancing in age and dealing with infirmities. Her Daddy's health was continuing to weaken. "...glad to hear that the hunting season had such beneficial effects on the touch of 'rheumatiz' that you had, Daddy."[187]

Mary Hester's letters continued to her parents and other family members at home. More and more they were typed. Often she would make multiple carbon copies of the same letter, jot personal notes on each one and send them to various family members and church contacts. These "carbonated" letters, as she so often called them, made it possible for

---

[186] Mary Hester Powell letter of February 9, 1958.
[187] Mary Hester Powell to J. C. Powell, October 27, 1957.

her to keep up with correspondence while also maintaining a heavy schedule of nursing and teaching. Even with hand-written letters, there were usually paragraphs scribbled around the margins as later additions - things she'd remembered to say. Often they were almost illegible.

Writing style was partially shaped by postage regulations. For many years a pre-printed, pre-stamped air mail form only a single sheet and on very thin paper went for reduced rates. Mary Hester Powell, along with almost all missionaries, crammed every word they could into every corner in order to use the forms without requiring additional postage.

Gradually more help was personally coming to Mary Hester and other missionaries from individual churches back home. For a time, she had someone who helped get out the correspondence. She wrote her thanks to "kind friends who have made it possible for me to write you again in this way. Never thought I'd be so 'posh' as to have a private secretary."[188]

Carlyle's older brother Halstead had moved to Rock Hill, South Carolina fairly early in his life. He worked with the railroad there. In the 1950's he donated land for the construction of a Baptist church. It was named

---

[188] May 25, 1958.

Powell Memorial. But the Powell who was honored was not Halstead, but his brother Carlyle ... for many years of mission service. In January 1960, Carlyle was on hand for the dedication of the church. The church changed its name to Oakwood Acres Baptist Church on December 12, 1978 and still serves its community.

Carlyle and Rosa spent considerable time in Rock Hill both on furlough and after retirement, including having a house there for a time. Friends and Nigerian students would refer to them as residents of Warsaw, Burgaw and Rock Hill.

Many missionaries were in regular contact with the Powells after retirement. One of them stood out to me: "I spent last weekend with your precious Mary Hester and Ruth Kube, and so enjoyed being with them! ... Mary Hester ... was so charming and pretty. I know that it is hard for you to live away from her, yet a joy to be able to give all that you have for the salvation of Nigeria.

"I was retired Dec. 1 and started home in January. I had five weeks in Philippines, two in Indonesia, a visit to Australia where I helped with personal work in the Billy Graham Crusade. Visited all of our stations in Malaya, had two days in Vietnam at Saigon, four days in Bangkok, a few in Burma, three weeks in India and on to Iran, Lebanon, Egypt, Holy Land, Turkey, Greece, Rome and here. Miss Knight and I fly for Rome the 15th and have six or eight weeks in Europe, reaching home about middle of September.

"I have been amazed at the immensity of Baptist work in this country. I had a tour of eleven stations with Miss [Josephine Anna] Scaggs and Aletha Fuller and a nurse friend of hers out from America - otherwise I could not have seen so much. I shall ever praise the Lord for the privilege. May you be kept in health and greatly used at home where your message is so needed. Most Sincerely Yours, Bertha Smith".[189]

Rosa and Carlyle continued to stay in touch with missionaries back in Nigeria and with national workers who had been introduced to Christian service during their years as missionaries. Frequently the letters they received from Nigeria thanked them for small amounts of money they had sent to help with educational or emergency needs. Sometimes the money had been sent by way of Mary Hester or through one of their missionary friends. It seems likely this dedicated couple continued to be involved in the spread of the Gospel abroad not only

---

[189] July 2, 1959.

through their own sacrificial giving from their meager retirement, but also with donations made through them by family and friends.

In October 1959, Mary Hester wrote her parents that staff at Ogbomoso were cleaning the new hospital and about to move in. For her part, she was finishing classes and then packing. She was moving to Eku.[190]

Ethel Rebecca Harmon wrote in evaluation for Rosa Powell's service record: "Few missionaries have been able to identify themselves with the African people as Mrs. Powell did. Her command of the Yoruba language and knowledge of the customs and mind of the people gave her an opening into the heart of the African that few have been able to attain." When it was learned their beloved teacher and principal was retiring and returning to the United States and probably would not be back to Nigeria, one student replied: "But she will have to come back. She is an African."

And they did return to Nigeria ... this time as honored guests of a newly independent nation.

---

[190] Mary Hester Powell to J. C. and Rosa Powell, October 15, 1959.

Powells with Grace Carson
and Dr. & Mrs. Geo. Stadler
Frances Jones Home
October 1960

## Chapter 14
## Independence

*Newspaper clippings still heralded the news*
*of the local family honored by a foreign government.*
*The Powells had been invited to return as honored*
*guests to their Nigeria.*

### A Colony Gains Independence

At midnight, October 1, 1960, Princess
Alexandria, Queen Elizabeth's representative
to Nigeria, handed over to the Prime Minister
of the Federation of Nigeria the constitutional
instrument by which Britain transferred
sovereignty to Nigeria. That ended 100 years of
British rule in the country.

The British had been training Nigerians
for independence almost from the moment
they began to pull together the warring tribes.
Independence, however, had not come easily.
For a long time the Northern region of Nigeria,
which was Muslim, had promised holy war
against the south. Reluctantly Sir Abubakar
Tafawa Balewa agreed to become the protector
of Northern interests in Lagos. On a 1955
river-travel fact-finding tour of America he
very suddenly realized the amazing results of
American democracy. He concluded if so many
people from so many countries could forge a

single, great nation, Nigeria could do it as well. In 1957, Sir Abubakar Tafawa Balewa became the first Prime Minister of Nigeria in a first step to prepare the way for Nigerian independence.

It was the regional government of Western Nigeria which made special invitation to Southern Baptist missionaries to come for the celebration of independence. That special invitation was proffered to the Powells, Sadlers and Miss May Edgel Perry.[191] It is likely that invitation would never have come had it not been for one governmental official.

Samuel Ladoke Akintola was born July 7, 1910 to a wealthy family who had been leaders in the Yoruba tribe's military for generations. Eventually he would become the eighth Oloye Aare Kakanfo - the ceremonial general of the Yoruba army. At the end of World War I, his father was unable to return to Nigeria for a time and Ladoke found himself living with his grandfather in Ogbomoso. There he attended Baptist Day School and later the Baptist College and Seminary. Having distinguished himself as a student, he was sent to Lagos as Tutor in General Science, Biology and Bible Knowledge at the Baptist Academy there. He served that position from 1930 until 1942. He was also a lay Baptist preacher.

---

[191] Letter of confirmation from H. Cornell Goerner to Rosa Powell, June 7, 1960.

While in Lagos, Ladoke met and eventually married (1935) Faderera Awomolo who had been trained as a nurse at Baptist Hospital, Ogbomoso. After his career in teaching, Akintola went on to journalism and then took a law degree in the UK. Returning to Nigeria, he helped found the Action Group and was soon deeply involved in politics. A conflict with Obafemi Awolowo began in the independence period and eventually led to a split in the party. By 1960, S. L. Akintola was emerging as the new premier of the Western Region of Nigeria. A distinct region of the country with primarily Yoruba population, the Western Region was a significant player in the emerging national government.

Akintola served as Premier of the Western Region from Nigerian Independence in October 1960 until January 1966 except for a six-month period when political challengers temporarily removed him from office only to have him restored by the courts. He was assassinated January 15, 1966 as a military junta took over the nation.

Debate has raged about the political excesses and abuses attributed to the later years of Akintola's life. Those are matters for historians in the world and especially in Nigeria to argue. What cannot be argued is the tremendous impact of Southern Baptist missionaries upon his and his wife's lives, his appreciation of missionaries and his Christian faith as shapers not only of his life, but of emerging Nigeria. One can only wonder if the history of late-century Nigeria would have been different had Akintola lived and emerged into national leadership. What difference might it have made for Christian missions in Nigeria if he had led the Nigerian government?

"According to Dr. Goerner, the Honorable S. L. Akintola, a product of Baptist schools, received two visitors in his home in Ogbomoso. One was an African journalist, the other a prominent government official from the Northern region. The journalist commented bitterly and critically about missionaries and missions in Africa.

"The official from the Northern region, a Muslim, said sharply to the journalist, 'It's the missionaries who helped bring education, propriety, and peace to the Western region. If we in the North had been wise, we would have invited them to help us long ago. Then we would have been much farther advanced than we are.'

"Mr. Akintola pointed to a nearby cemetery. 'Do you see that grave yonder? There lies Miss Lucile Reagan, a Baptist missionary. All I am today I owe to her and to her associates.

"Many times during the celebration for Nigerian Independence, this same Honorable Chief S. L. Akintola paid tribute to Christian missions for the part they played in the development of the country and making independence possible. In a T.V. interview with Dr. Sadler, this man asked Dr. Sadler how long Baptists would continue their ministry in the country and Dr. Sadler answered 'Just as long as Nigerians want us.'"[192]

By 1960, Carlyle Powell was suffering with advancing Parkinson's Disease. His sisters worried he was not up to the trip. But they knew he would not be dissuaded. "At least," they said, "if he doesn't survive the trip, he'll die happy."[193]

A newspaper article with picture in *The (Wilmington NC) Morning Star* for September 23, 1960 reported: "Miss Mary Hester Powell left Wilmington by plane Friday for E'ku via Sapele, Nigeria, where she will resume work as supervisor-instructor at the Baptist School of Nursing there. Accompanying her are her parents, the Rev. & Mrs. J. C. Powell, of

---

[192] Hand written notes on the Independence Celebration by Rosa Powell.
[193] Personal notes of Mary Hester Powell.

Warsaw, who were missionaries in Nigeria from 1919-1955. The Powells were invited to Nigeria for two months as guests of the government as an expression of appreciation for their long service."

In the bulletin of Warsaw Baptist Church for July 24, 1960, Pastor Delamar Parkerson wrote: "We believe that this invitation made [not] by the Nigerian Baptists, but by the Nigerian government, is sufficient evidence of the tremendous impact of their lives and message in Nigeria."

Independence was more than the one-day affair. Celebrations lasted off and on for weeks in various parts of the country. The journey to Nigeria for Independence resulted in a wonderful homecoming opportunity for the Powells who traveled to several towns and villages.

The Independence Celebration went smoothly and peacefully. Mary Hester wrote a circular letter to her friends reporting Independence in Nigeria had come without incident, in contrast with what had happened in the Congo. "Everywhere we've been, and all we've heard about, has given credit to the Christian missions and gratitude to the foresight of the British government in preparing Nigeria for the smooth transition which has taken place so far."[194]

Dr. H. Cornell Goerner, Secretary for Africa, Europe, and the Near East, spent months living in Nigeria in the period right after independence. He wrote in a report contrasting Nigeria with other African nations with larger European populations: "Nigeria is now an independent African nation, with Europeans, who number less than 1 in 2,000, present in the country only as guests and visitors who have a service to render to the African people." In another place he said: "On the one hand, there is a sense of gratitude for the achievements of the past century of mission work, amazement at the rapid progress now going on, and conviction that the responsibility in the future must pass more and more into the hands of Nigerian leadership. On the other hand, there is the overwhelming sense of need, the enormity of the unfinished task, and the conviction that the day of the missionary has by no means ended. Missionaries are still needed, still wanted, and still more overworked than ever."[195]

The Nigerian government was supposed to pay for the Powell's trip. As late as March 2, 1961, Ira Newberne Patterson was

---

[194] October 24, 1960.
[195] A copy of this report carried no date.

writing the Powells the government had not paid for the daily incidentals and the Executive Committee of the Mission had voted to cover those expenses themselves. He also noted receipt of a gift of $200 from the Powells and indicated the money would be put to use in part for the education of a national pastor's son.

## Back in Nigeria

From 1960 through 1962 Mary Hester was at Baptist Hospital Eku working in their School of Nursing. The First Baptist Church in Eku was started in 1926 by J. E. Aganbi. In 1935 Dr. William H. Carson arrived in the area to further the mission work. Once a month a physician came from Sapele to help the sick. It was not until 1945 and the coming of Rev. E. Milford and Mrs. Eleanor Kathrine Howell that plans were made to open a hospital at Eku and the dispensary was opened under the hand of Mrs. Howell. New buildings were finished in 1949 and the hospital was dedicated on July 27, 1950 with 32 beds available. Dr. Paul Shelby Cullen, M. D. arrived that year and completed the water and electrical systems and set up a laboratory. In 1960 further land was acquired and buildings completed.[196]

The Nigerian Baptist Convention had sent out its own first foreign missionary a few months before independence in 1960. The coming of independence accelerated the "indigenizing" of the country. Missionaries would learn that word and a whole new way of doing missions.

Independence meant there was opportunity to help shape the relationship between state and church. Mary Hester wrote that a political candidate had stayed over at the compound and had breakfast. In the conversation, he had asked "why Baptists had not accepted government aid for their hospitals. We were glad to ... answer that one, saying that where government money went, control followed in its wake - also ... we needed some institutions where we could attempt to train Christian leaders.... Besides all that, we didn't think it fair for the government to subsidize *any* religion.... I 'lowed as how it was worth something of a scramble on Sunday night to have a chance on Monday morning to help the Parliamentary Secretary to the Premier of the Western Region to understand

---

[196] "Eku Baptist Hospital - Past, Present, Future" - a three-page, typed timeline of the hospital prepared for the 1990 Fortieth Anniversary Celebration.

the Baptist position on separation of church and state a little better."[197]

An independent Nigerian government soon began to expand its expectations of educational and health institutions. Mary Hester wrote, "The educational people are all upset because the Ministry of Education says so many of our teacher training colleges have to be upgraded *immediately* or close. ... Christian Workers' Board is all set to ask for grants for all."[198] The grants would have been governmental grants to assist with upgrades.

But the need for Baptist work continued to be intense. Hospitals and the nurses to staff them were in especially great demand. A carbon letter from "Bill and Leslie"[199] on January 18, 1962 reported 3300 had applied for entrance to the Nursing School (Ogbomoso?), 400 would sit for entrance exams, but there was space in the program for only 20 new students.

---

[197] Mary Hester Powell at Eku Hospital to "folk", November 12, 1961.

[198] Mary Hester Powell to J. C. and Rosa Powell, August 20, 1961.

[199] William Jackson Williams, M. D. and Leslie Sands Williams.

## A Church Come Alongside

Published in the weekly bulletin of First
Baptist Church, Wilmington North Carolina
for February 4, 1962 is recognition by Mary
Hester Powell of the donations of the church to
benefit their chapel. FBC had long made Mary
Hester *their* missionary and had come
alongside her in a variety of ways to support
her mission work through prayer and
donations: "...I stopped to do some shopping in
Ibadan, and personally saw the organ loaded
on to the hospital lorry along with the pulpit
stand and chairs for the chapel. I got in the day
after it did and heard that staff and students of
the nursing school were more than pleased.
The students wanted to 'sing to it' right away.
It has a beautiful tone and I believe it will be
highly satisfactory. It has foot pedals to pump,
which I know sounds old fashioned; but our
light plant goes on the blink too regularly for
us to risk an electric one, especially when the
doctor who is acting superintendent and chief
engineer is going home on furlough right
away! Any volunteer for maintenance men?
We need them too!

"When I reached home I found the letter
and check for $154.00 for screens which I'll turn
over to the business manager in the A.M.

"You folks have been more than generous, and we're all grateful. I just hope our witness in this land will match your love and concern." First Baptist Church had helped Mary Hester in many ways, including underwriting her salary for a time on the field. All their support had been done through the Foreign Mission Board in respect to Board policy and the Cooperative Program agreements.

## Emergency Back Home

After retirement, Carlyle's health declined quickly. In July 1961, Mary Hester wrote to H. Cornell Goerner at the Foreign Mission Board that her Daddy had surgery in Winston-Salem (Baptist Hospital), but was recovering. Goerner wrote back he had called Warsaw and spoken with Rosa. Carlyle had experienced an attack of pleurisy after discharge and ended up back in the hospital for a time before being discharged again.

A letter written to Goerner from a Warsaw doctor shed a lot of light on Carlyle's serious state: "I am writing you at the request of Mrs. J. C. Powell to inform you as to her husband's physical condition. Julius Carlyle Powell (patient) has been a total invalid for the past 12 months. As you know, Mr. Powell has been retired from the Board some years now due to physical disability. He is suffering from advanced arteriosclerosis. Even though this is generalized, the cerebral vessels are hardened to the extent that the patient has developed severe mental confusion. He is disoriented a great deal of the time and mentally confused generally. He is unable to dress and undress himself without assistance. He has complete loss of speech at times. In the past year he has had two major operations. He is now in the hospital recovering from herniotomy.

"It is not possible, of course, to say how long Mr. Powell can continue living but we can say with certainty that he will not improve. I would say that it is possible for him to live another year. On the other hand, his condition is such that he might pass away any time."[200]

A letter immediately came to Rosa from the Board, but written by Baker James Cauthen, himself. Goerner was away and the doctor's letter had been forwarded to Cauthen. He assured her the Foreign Mission Board would cover expenses for medical care and for nursing care if needed. He would send a copy of his letter and that of Dr. Straughan to Mary Hester with his own urging she schedule her

---

[200] Dr. J. W. Straughan, Warsaw to Dr. Cornell Goerner at the Foreign Mission Board, March 29, 1962.

furlough early unless an emergency necessitated her returning immediately.

Rosa wrote Cauthen back on April 11. Carl was again in the hospital, this time for pneumonia. If Mary Hester was coming at all, she should come now.

Mary Hester wrote home on April 7, "Uncle J. D. [Chambers] I know you've been a lot of company for Daddy. I'm so glad this last hospitalization is over, Daddy, and hope that you won't have any more trouble now. Let's steer clear of abscesses and the like - they're a nuisance, to say the very least. I hope you're on your feet again - but don't overdo them; they're right delicate little things, you know." Obviously the mail lag had kept her from the most current information.

Although her furlough wasn't supposed to start until August of 1963, Mary Hester wrote to friends from Warsaw that she had arrived April 29, 1962 on furlough early because of her Dad's illness. He was improving, able to come to the table and sit up to watch TV. He was going for rides in the car, but going up and down steps was still a challenge.

"Some thought he [J. C.] might not live until Mary Hester could get here. Others

thought that if he did live that long he might
not be able to recognize her. Thank the Lord,
Carl was at home, came home the day before
she arrived, and has amazed the people with
his improvement. Getting home and her
coming have done much, but God has
graciously heard and answered the prayers of
people everywhere."[201]

For the hospital stay, the Foreign
Mission Board would pick up the cost of
$618.93, leaving the Powells with only $100.00
in expenses.

A note from Mary Hester on June 29,
1962 indicated her Daddy had been in the
hospital for the fifth time, this time with
pneumonia, but was home. "It takes at least
two people to turn him in bed or to get him up
for brief periods in a chair by the bed. How
mother managed alone for so long I don't see."

Eventually "Sky" Powell did regain a
measure of health. In June of 1963, Mary
Hester typed a letter that circulated to friends:
"Daddy's general health improved so during
last summer that he was able to go to church,
walk the block to his sister's house, and even to
enjoy several of the local high school football
games. He was 'tickled pink' when the
cheerleaders gave him a season's ticket to all

[201] Rosa Powell to Baker James Cauthen, May 16, 1962.

home games ... for being such a faithful supporter! ... In late October, he fell, breaking his hip."

In late 1962. Mary Hester wrote to H. Cornell Goerner her Daddy had a pin put in.[202] It would be a long recovery complicated by a kidney infection in April 1963. On May 26, 1963, Mary Hester would write again to Goerner the doctor had said her Daddy could put some weight on his hip. She observed he had not put weight on either foot since the fall and would have to learn to walk again.

### Visit From Ezekiel

The missionary may leave the field, but the people do not forget the missionary.

Ezekiel Ojo came into the Powells' lives as a young boy whom the missionaries helped by paying his school fees. In exchange he did small chores for the couple and on the school farm. During a furlough, Carlyle and Rosa received word the boy had been missing from school. One of the missionaries had gone to his village and discovered Ezekiel had been sold into slavery to pay off medical bills for his sick father. Thanks to that missionary and the help of a police officer who had been her student,

---

[202] Letter of November 3, 1962.

the family who had purchased the boy was found and persuaded to give him his freedom. The Powells continued to pay his school costs.

Ezekiel not only finished school in Nigeria, but also one year of University at Ibadan. In 1968, he journeyed to the Untied States to enroll at Oklahoma Baptist University in Shawnee.

On August 29, 1971, he wrote a letter to all three of the Powells and addressed Rosa and Carlyle as "Mother" and "Father." He thanked them for the gift, but asked them not to send money anymore as he was sure they could use it themselves. He reported to them he was working in the library during sessions and in the maintenance department during holidays to pay for what his scholarships did not cover. He enclosed a picture of his wife and family back in Nigeria, separated from him for many months and by many miles. "I desire to visit you all some day and I am thinking and praying about it - if it should be the Lord's will I'll be very glad if I can make it - say next December. Before I left Nigeria I told the Shaki Association that I would try to visit for all. I did not realize how great the U.S. is and the distance of one state to the other."

Ezekiel graduated from OBU with a major in sociology and a minor in education.

He continued his education at Oklahoma State University in Agricultural Education. In 1973, while in his masters' program at OSU, Ezekiel finally made the trip to see Carlyle and Rosa in Warsaw. He saw poultry and hog farms in Duplin County, played Nigerian games and showed African souvenirs to the Royal Ambassadors at Warsaw Baptist Church. Mostly, he got to see his beloved Powells, especially the invalid "Sky" Powell a little over a year before the missionary's death.

Several years later, a missionary friend of Rosa Powell's was visiting a village in Nigeria and asked a kind man to help her bargain to buy a straw hat. Instead of purchasing one hat, he bought two and asked her to send one to Mrs. Powell. Ezekiel Ojo was home teaching agriculture in Nigeria.[203]

## Continued Contact

Letters came regularly to the Powells from other missionaries and from natives they had known, led to Christ or ordained to service. The Powells also sent regular donations of money to individual Nigerian Christian workers.

---

[203] Pieced together from newspaper clippings reclaimed from the Powell House.

Mary Hester continued to advocate for missionary nurses. "I've felt for several years - especially since independence - that our days in Nigeria are limited." She went on to talk of the need to raise up a generation of well-trained, local nurses.[204]

From her return to the States in 1962, Mary Hester had first extended her furlough and then gone on inactive status. On November 19, 1968, H. Cornell Goerner wrote her suggesting she go ahead and resign and seek reappointment later if she were able to return to the field. He indicated having too many missionaries on inactive status might hinder recruitment. He also suggested she not tell Carlyle. Her resignation was tendered and the Board accepted it on December 5, 1968.

When figuring service from appointment to retirement or resignation, the full service of the Powells would technically be 93 years. But Mary Hester always figured her service to 1962 when she returned to Warsaw. When 15-year pins were being awarded, Mary Hester objected since she had not been on the field the full time. "We definitely want you to have the fifteen year pin," Goerner wrote, "since you were under appointment all of that time, and you really deserve this. You almost

---

[204] Mary Hester Powell to H. Cornell Goerner, March 29, 1963.

made the twenty year pin before your resignation was accepted."[205]

## The Conclusion of Lives Well Lived

Like many, Kathleen Powell Snyder wrote the same basic Christmas message on all her cards each year. I found a never-mailed card from 1973 which read in part: "Our family is passing away rapidly now, only four of Mama's and Dads 12 children left. Carlyle is a helpless invalid, Annie Kate has not been able to turn herself in bed or feed herself a bite for over seven years, and is almost blind and very deaf...."

As for Rosa, Carlyle and Mary Hester, their lives settled into a restricted routine. In a Christmas time note to friends in 1968, Mary Hester reported her Daddy was walking with a walker, at least in his room. He would go outside in his wheelchair and could get to church some. She was working three shifts per week at Duplin General Hospital on the 3:00 to 11:00 shift and was singing in the church choir.

The family enlisted help when it was available. Woody, a high school boy, would come around after school to wheel Carlyle out

---

[205] H. Cornell Goerner to Mary Hester Powell, January 22, 1970.

of the house to play Parcheesi when his health permitted.

Once, at the end of one of his many hospital stays and when it looked like he might miss the last game of the high school football season, Carlyle was eager to be released. Special arrangements had to be made to get him to the game on a stretcher. Friends from Warsaw Baptist Church arranged with the local funeral home to use the "black car," usually reserved for use as a hearse, to convey him to the game on a stretcher. It was the talk of Warsaw for a long time, and is still recalled with a smile by those who remember.

Health problems were a regular challenge for Carlyle and required ongoing attention and care giving from Rosa and Mary Hester. Bouts with pneumonia in the fall of 1967 and again at Thanksgiving 1969 furthered his decline.

Rosa and Carlyle's 50th wedding anniversary in 1969 was turned into a Powell and Hocutt event. Members of the families came from far and wide for the occasion.

Despite his many and serious maladies, Carlyle outlived everyone's expectations. On March 26, 1974 he preceded his Rosa to another far shore. Rev. Boyce Brooks, Pastor of Warsaw

Baptist Church, did the funeral. H. Cornell Goerner represented the Foreign Mission Board. Mr. Owolabi and Mr. Bamikole from Nigeria brought remarks. Burial was at Pinecrest Cemetery in Warsaw. A recording of the service was taken back to Nigeria. In his will he left the Foreign Mission Board $1,700.

In December of 1974 an invitation came to Mary Hester from the Foreign Mission Board. Davis Saunders wrote asking her to consider returning to Africa, this time to Mbeye, Tanzania. The chronic shortage of missionary nurses meant they were without a nurse there.

It was a while before Mary Hester responded. She wrote she had considered going back to the field, but her mother seemed more feeble and accident prone than she had expected. Reluctantly, she turned down the offer. "Another complicating factor... is that I'm an only child. Mother has a sister across the street and Daddy's two sisters are next door, one of whom is a total invalid."[206]

Rosa Hocutt Powell once more joined her "Carl" on that far shore June 13, 1982. There was a memorial service on June 15. Rosa had asked there be no spoken word. The brief

---

[206] Mary Hester Powell to Davis and Mary Saunders, April 22, 1975

eulogy by Rev. John A. Johnson was that - brief. A great deal of scripture was read.

Mary Hester Powell continued at her home in Warsaw for many years. She eventually retired from nursing. For many years she was a beloved Sunday School teacher at Warsaw Baptist Church. One of her class members remembers Mary Hester as very knowledgeable of Bible names and geography. When folks of the church were sick, she would always bring them Jello. No cook, she was still there with her "dish" before anyone else, often beating the pastor to see them.

As old age began to claim her vitality and at the encouragement of her cousins and church family, Mary Hester searched out a life-care community in Greenville, North Carolina. At this writing she has celebrated her 96th birthday and continues with clear mind and remarkable vitality to talk of Jesus... and of Nigeria.

# Chapter 15
# Words From "Sky" Powell

*I laid my head down on my desk. It had been a 3:30 morning, but that wasn't the reason. I'd been pouring through a large cardboard box of papers loaned to me by Mary Hester Powell. When I'd picked them up, I'd thought they were manuscript pages. But Mary Hester said she wasn't aware her Dad did any writing particularly. But there before me were four separate writing projects "Sky" Powell had pushed to completion, though he'd never published them. I knew, with some measure of exhaustion, my own project had just gotten much larger.*

## Impressions of Nigeria

In a letter to Charles Maddry, Carlyle Powell talked about rewriting a manuscript he'd done on religions in Africa. He acknowledged that although he'd counted 410 Yoruba religions he thought he'd only accounted for one-third of the total.[207]

While still a young missionary, in his second tour of duty, Carlyle Powell knew he needed something to give the churches back in the United States to answer their questions. He began to write out what he observed in Nigeria.

---

[207] J. C. Powell to Charles Maddry, June 11, 1935.

In the 1930s some of those observations were written into letters to Mary Hester when she began to ask about their first experiences in-country. Apparently he never found a publisher for the accounts. Instead, a rough manuscript found its way into storage where it was forgotten - even by Mary Hester.

When I discovered "Sky" Powell's writings and began to wade through them, I knew this book needed to find the light of day. Not only was it important primary source material for the biography I was writing, it also cast insight on developing Nigeria and the social and religious dynamics still impacting the country, the continent and the world.

I determined this manuscript had to be published first. It required a full rewrite to make it publication ready. Many quotes from the rewritten manuscript are included in the chapters of this book.

Under the title *Impressions of Nigeria*, Carlyle Powell's reflections on the country, its people, customs and religion are now available in print and digital format from Amazon.com.

## 112 Questions and Answers on Deaconship

In a letter to Maddry on August 24, 1938 Carlyle indicated he'd gotten back the manuscript of 100 questions on deaconship. "...all these questions have been asked me in dead seriousness."

"I have gathered these from questions that have been asked me on the deaconship for the past five years." He'd had them printed himself. Copies with covers cost 3 cents each, without covers, 2 cents each.[208]

*112 Questions and Answers on Deaconship in Baptist Churches As Touching Problems in Nigeria* organizes the questions into subjects including qualifications, jurisdiction, authority, privileges, expelling, and retiring from office. There were several separate sections on the role, function and qualifications of the deaconess. The booklet was printed in both English and Yoruba. In a foreword to the booklet, Powell wrote: "In the year 1935 I saw that our churches needed to be properly organized by having deacons ordained in them. So I put out 100 questions and answers concerning the Deacon. I had these questions published in our own paper, the *Nigerian Baptist*. I have here rearranged these in logical order and added 12 more that were handed in

---

[208] J. C. Powell to Charles to Maddry, January 4, 1939.

at our last Associational meeting at Tede." This booklet is not currently in print. Copies are in my possession, at the International Mission Board and the Powell Room of Warsaw Baptist Church.

"Instead of having a deacon body, most of the mission churches had a church committee. Sometimes that committee was poorly manned and sometimes it overstepped what would normally have been acceptable authority for a congregationally governed church, but it proved absolutely necessary to have that group in place to help guide the congregation."[209]

## One Gross of Thoughts About the Master

Carlyle published a second booklet to clarify Nigerian Baptist's understanding of Jesus Christ. Entitled *One Gross of Thoughts About the Master*, he organized the 144 statements (without biblical references this time) into 12 "packages" of 12 thoughts each:

[An Introduction of 12 things]
12 Things He Is
12 Things He Did That
    No One Else Can Do
12 Things He Expects of Me

---

[209] Powell, *Impressions*, 88.

12 Things He Cannot Do
12 Things He Never Did Do
12 National Defects He Does Not Like
12 Things He and I Can Do
12 Questionable Things
    He Turns Back On Us
12 Things That Show Me
    He Is the Messiah
12 Indirect Proofs of His Divinity
12 Messages After Death

This booklet was only in English and printed by Advent Press. At the end of each of the 12 "packages" of thoughts was an original poem by Carlyle. This booklet is not currently in print. Copies are in my possession, at the International Mission Board and the Powell Room of Warsaw Baptist Church.

## Thirty-Six Questions

Powell published a half-sheet tract entitled "Thirty-six Questions With Biblical Background." Although there is no date on the piece, it was apparently used in classes conducted for new believers in advance of their baptism. The tract was only in English. Some of the questions included:

"1. Are you a sinner?
2. Are you trusting Christ for salvation?

4. Who saved you?

5. What is the *orisha* of your
    father's house?

6. Why have you left these *orishas*?

7. Can *orishas* save you?

9. Who is Jesus?

19. Can baptism save you?

20. Why are you asking for baptism?

25. Have you a concubine?

28. Have you a secret wife?

29. What will you do if your people die
    and leave you a wife?

36. Are you willing to sign the
    following pledge

(a) I promise in the presence of God and man never to have a concubine, never to take a second wife while my first wife lives, never to have more than one living wife at a time.

(b) If my people die and leave me a second wife I will refuse her and give her her freedom in court without claim of dowry.

(c) If I fail to keep the above pledge I will withdraw from the Baptist Church and bring no reproach on her honour with my immoral life."

This tract is not currently in print.

## Translation and Commentaries

Though he struggled with the Yoruba language early on, Carlyle Powell emerged with a fine grasp of the tribal language. He was asked to translate the New Testament book of Acts into the Yoruba language. In the end, he not only translated Acts, but wrote a commentary on the book.

Carlyle's work on Acts as well as commentaries on selected Pauline epistles began early on. He wrote on February 20, 1928 he was working on Philemon and Philippians in Yoruba and had finished Acts and sent it to the committee.

Rough manuscripts of commentaries on Galatians, Ephesians, Philippians, Colossians and Philemon exist today. None has ever been published. The possibility of bringing them to publication in some form is currently under consideration.

## Christ the Center of All Things

Carlyle produced an article, probably never published, entitled "Jesus: A Man Among Men and the Savior of Men." In the article, he wrote "I accept it with my whole heart, and believe it with my whole mind, and am willing to live my life in any kind of circumstances to convince men of its truth."

Powell expressed his very practical Christology in a book entitled *Christ the Center of All Things*. In the 1940s he sought a publisher and circulated a manuscript of it particularly to Baptist publishing houses. On May 22, 1945, Hight C. Moore of the Baptist Sunday School Board wrote Carlyle a three-page, handwritten letter in which he reviewed the manuscript. Biblical, sound, and likely to be well taken by a receptive reader, he still believed the book would be better served if it came from a publisher with a narrower audience.

Carlyle did not find a publisher for the manuscript. The rough manuscript of this book still exists and I have concluded it needs publication. The author's missionary career as well as some decades of impact should cause us to take a closer look at the faith in Christ that drove a farm boy to Africa. Future publication to be determined, but likely.

## Devotionals

Also under review by Hight Moore in his 1945 letter was a collection of devotionals put together for every day of the year. Moore lamented the huge amount of devotional literature pouring from the presses in those days as he also turned down that project.

In his retirement days, "Sky" Powell published some of these devotionals in *The Duplin Times*, the local newspaper, on a semi-regular basis at least during 1965. Here is an example of the devotionals which I am in the process of rewriting:

-------------

January 1
THE GREAT JOINER

*Isn't this the carpenter's son?*
Matthew 13:55 (NIV)

He was the son of poor, working parents. Now he has become the parent and friend of all poor working people. Moffatt translated the reference *"Is this not the son of the joiner?"* thus referring to Joseph with a carpenter's function as the joiner of pieces of wood.

Jesus was also the Son of the Great Joiner - one who spliced heaven and earth together in peace and love and mutual understanding.

Christ did not sit on the throne and command us to slave unaided, for he was born of poor working parents and joined-up with us in hard labor himself. He became a co-laborer with Joseph, his foster father, and later became earth's soul winner. If taken as a partner, he will always lighten our task. He is a Lord who knows the work we have in hand, and one who lends a hand in the work we have to do. Truly we can say he has become the parent and friend of all poor working people.

Just as he has taken the task for the years
To join heaven and earth together in love,
So come let us begin each day of this year
With Jesus our friend and guide from above.

Lord Jesus, come into this life of mine,
For in shame it often turns away from Thee.
Help me in Thee alone to find,
The one like whom I would have myself be.
---------------

These devotionals for the entire year are being published in four volumes under the title *A Year With "Sky" Powell*. Volume 1 is expected to be released by year's end 2018.

**Poetry**

"Sky" Powell wrote many poems. When he wrote his devotionals, especially, he would almost inevitably conclude them with a poem.

His writing style was in simple meter with constant efforts to rhyme. The result often feels forced. Nevertheless, the content of those poems reveal a great deal about his faith, basic doctrine and the ardor of his beliefs.

At the end of his article entitled "Jesus: A Man Among Men and the Savior of Men" was this poem obviously meant to be a hymn:

### Let's Risk All In the Hands of Jesus

I am told in the old, old story,
That Jesus lived a man among men;
Robbed himself of heavenly glory,
To become our redeemer from sin;

chorus: Let's risk all in the hands of Jesus,
For he never forsakes a friend;
Though it may seem to us mysterious,
No one else can forgive our sins.

Though the Son of the King of Glory,
Some would make him only a man;
These change neither him nor his story,
For these are the works of God's hands.

They would steal in trying to rob him -
Take from him his honor and crown;
But they'll never draw me from him,
For in him alone was my pardon found.

The typed copy of another poem has a notation by Carlyle Powell saying he had written it in 1916 while a student at Wake Forest College:

Out here in the woods all alone
I have found a flower snug in its nook.
Now I see the world is its home,
The hills its tower and nature its book.

Little herb may I tell what I see
Written on your leaves so fair?
Just a verse or a line it will be,
For none with your beauty can compare.

What care I for yon ugly city
With her towering walls and crowded streets
When your beauty by men yet untold
Lies all enraptured here at my feet?

You are the blush of nature's cheek.
Your fragrance you give back to the air.
Ah ... well, then ... your secret I'll keep
In my heart a token near ... so rare.

### "Because Susan Prayed"

[Let Mary Hester Powell have a word here. On July 15, 1958 she wrote a letter to her Mother and Daddy on the back of a carbon of this story. She'd written it originally to go into children's missions magazines to express the importance of the nursing mission. Mary Hester also, in her retirement years, did occasional articles for her retirement community newsletter in which she reflected upon missionary service and recalled specific incidents.]

"Are there any requests for prayer?"

The voice was that of Dr. Goldie[210] from the Leprosy Service who was just closing his devotional at the regular Thursday station prayer meeting.

Susan's mother spoke up: "Susan would like for us to remember a little girl at the hospital whose arm is to be operated on tomorrow - and she'll have to stay in bed for four or five whole weeks!"

Four weeks was a long time - just *how* long Susan very well knew, for only that very afternoon she had had a cast taken off her own arm. It had been on for four weeks, too.

Susan had swung on a rope hanging from a high limb on a tall, tall igba tree in her front yard, and had cracked the bone near her shoulder. It had hurt awfully badly at the time, and having a cast on was most inconvenient!

---

[210] Robert Frederick Goldie, M. D.

No more swinging from the rope - you just couldn't do it one-handedly very well- and that wasn't quite fair because Stinson (who was just older) could still swing - with two hands!

Mother had had to bathe her - just as if she were no bigger than Edna Rachel - and Edna Rachel was just five! Once she had slipped in the tub, cast and all!

It was hard to get comfortable at night, too. You either had to sit up, or prop up your arm on a pillow - or both; and it was hard to turn. Besides, whoever heard of sleeping without lying down, or even turning over.

All in all, four weeks was a *long* time.

As the prayers were prayed, both silent and out loud, the missionaries and Susan remembered Susan's little friend.

The next day Titi (short for Titilayo, pronounced *Tee-tee-lay-yaw*) went to sleep quickly and easily, even though the ether didn't smell good at all. She woke up just as easily, to see a nurse standing over her, asking her if she knew where she was.

"Hos-pee-tul," Titi answered sleepily, and promptly dozed off again.

Big tears filled her eyes later as she realized her elbow was hurting her. It was strung up in traction with a metal pin through her elbow and weights to hold it in place. Her hand was in a sling. Dr. Williams[211] said she wasn't to sit up, either.

Soon a nurse came with some medicine to ease her pain, and Titi smiled.

Susan and her brother and sister took toys and books for Titi to play with. Titi liked those, especially the blocks that made three sets of pictures. Titi didn't like it, though, when the woman who had been in the next bed stole some of her blocks to take home to her child! That woman was not a Christian. Titi knew Christians didn't behave like that, because her mother and father were Christians, and she wanted to be one too.

Four weeks wasn't so long after all, though, because Susan had prayed for her.

---

[211] William Jackson Williams, M. D.

## The Powell Project

The conclusion of this biography now appears only the beginning. "The Powell Project" is a larger body of work necessitated by Carlyle Powell's pen that refused to remain still and a missionary heart that could not be retired. Not only *Impressions of Nigeria*, already out, but also the devotionals have to find light of day. And there is *Christ the Center of All Things* and maybe even the commentaries. Then there are the hundreds of photographs that need to be preserved. I encourage you to join me for the rest of this journey as it unfolds.

Let "Sky" Powell, himself, offer more words before the close of this book.

### Oh Lord, With Me Abide

Why should I cowardly displease my Lord,
And bring grief to all His heavenly host;
By trying to battle with my human sword,
Instead of hiding in the Holy Ghost?

I would center my mind on things above,
My own wayward pathway let me not take;
I would arm in arm walk with Thee in love,
So that I may never Thy law forsake.

Lord, live within me and increase my faith,
Let Thy Spirit control my every thought;
Then shall I bring to Thee sinners in haste,
For they by Thy blood are already bought.

Why should I do myself this countless wrong,
Failing hourly to have Thee by my side?
Lord, help me in my heart to sing this song,
"In life, in death, O Lord, with me abide."

- J. C. Powell (Warsaw)[212]

The urgency with which J. C. Powell concluded his descriptions of Nigeria are also a useful end to this biographical treatment: "These people are losing confidence in their heathen gods and are going to turn to another form of religion. Shall it be Christ or Mohammed?"[213]

*We'd decided weeks before we were not the ones to restore the Powell House, but could anyone be found who would. It was a huge house. We'd advertised and shown it. Then suddenly a couple from out of town ... a showing ... an offer on the spot. The closing took place six days later. Teresa and I sat at home reflecting on the whirlwind of the whole experience of our three-month-ownership of the house. "You know, the only reason God led us to*

---

[212] Typed copy found in genealogical records.
[213] Powell, Impressions, 97.

*that house was so you could get the materials out to write this book." I looked at her and nodded. She's perceptive about these things.*

## Time Line

January 22, 1890 . . . . Julius Carlyle Powell born
September 27, 1891. . Rosa Beatrice Hocutt born
1904 . . . . . . . . . . . . . . . . . . .Carlyle's conversion
1910. . . . . . . . . . . . Carlyle ordained to ministry
        at Evergreen Baptist Church, Delway, NC
1912. . . . Rosa and Carlyle graduate Dell School
1914-1928. . . . . . . . . . . . . James Franklin Love
    Executive Secretary of Foreign Mission Board
1916. . . .Carlyle graduates Wake Forest College
1916-1917. . . . . . . . . Carlyle pastor at Snow Hill
            and Freemont Baptist churches
1917. . . . . . . .Rosa graduates Meredith College
1918. . . . . . . . . . . . . Rosa teaches at Dell School
1919. . . . Rosa teaches at James Sprunt Institute
1919. . . . . . . . . . . . . . . Carlyle graduates from
    The Southern Baptist Theological Seminary
June 11, 1919. . . . . . . . . . . . . . Carlyle and Rosa
                appointed missionaries by
        Southern Baptist Foreign Mission Board
July 24, 1919. . . . . . . Rosa and Carlyle married
1920 - 1933. . . . . . . .Carlyle assumes position as
                field missionary - Oyo, Nigeria
1920 - 1933. . . . . . . . . Rosa begins mission work
                    as women's worker

May 21, 1922. . . . . . . Mary Hester Powell born
Oyo, Nigeria
March 2, 1923 - March 22, 1924 . . . . . . Furlough
May 19, 1927 - August 18, 1928 . . . . . . Furlough
1928-1931 . . . . . Rosa teaches at Oyo Day School
1929-1932 . . . . . . . . . . . . . . . . . . T. Bronson Ray
Executive Secretary of Foreign Mission Board
July 12, 1931 - May 11, 1933 . . . . . . . . . Furlough
1933-1944 . . . . . . . . . . . . . . . Charles E. Maddry
Secretary of Foreign Mission Board
1933-1945 . . . . . . . . . . . . . . . . . Carlyle serves as
field missionary - Shaki, Nigeria
1933-1940 . . . . . . . . . . . . . . . . . Rosa teaches at
Elam Memorial Girl's School, Shaki, Nigeria
1934-1938 . . . . . . . . . . . . Mary Hester Powell at
Buies Creek Academy
(Later Campbell University)
March 15, 1936 - April 27, 1937 . . . . . . Furlough
1938-1942 . . . . . . . . . . . . . . Mary Hester Powell
at Meredith College
April 11, 1940 - March 15, 1941 . . . . . . Furlough
April 17, 1941 . . . . . . . Sinking of the steamship
Zamzam
1941-1945 . . . . . . . . . . . . Rosa serves as worker
with women and day schools - Shaki, Nigeria
1942. . Mary Hester graduates Meredith College
1942-1944 . . . . . . . . . . . . . . Mary Hester teaches
public school in Kinston, NC
(Social Science at Southwood High School)
1944-1953 . . . . . . . . . . . . . . . . M. Theron Rankin
Executive Secretary of Foreign Mission Board

1944-1945 . . . . . . . . . Mary Hester a receptionist
at doctor's office, Warsaw
1945-1948 . . . . . . . . . . . . . . Mary Hester Powell
at Johns Hopkins School of Nursing
March 9, 1944 - May 29, 1945 . . . . . . . . Furlough
1946-1952 . . . . . . . . . . . . . . . . . Carlyle serves as
field missionary in Oyo
1946-1947 . . . . . . . . . . . . . . . . . . . Rosa principal
at Oyo Baptist Boys' High School
1948 . . . Mary Hester graduates Johns Hopkins
University School of Nursing
1948 . . . . . . . . . . . . . .Mary Hester a staff nurse,
Johns Hopkins delivery floor
1948-1949 Mary Hester an office nurse, Warsaw
May 1, 1948 - May 18, 1949 . . . . . . . . .Furlough
1949 . . . . Mary Hester appointed for three-year
term as medical missionary to Nigeria
1949-1955 . . . . . . . . . . . . . Mary Hester Nurse in
Charge at Ogbomosho Baptist Hospital
1949-1952 . . . . . . . . . . . Rosa again principal at
Oyo Baptist Boys' High School
April 18, 1952 - June 20, 1953 . . . . . . . .Furlough
1953-1955 . . . . . . . . . . Rosa and Carlyle both at
Language and Orientation School
1954-1955 . . . . . . Mary Hester Nurse in Charge
at Ogbomosho Children's Home
1954-1979 . . . . . . . . . . . . . . Baker James Cauthen
Executive Secretary of Foreign Mission Board
November 30, 1956 . . . . . . . . Rosa and Carlyle
retire from mission service
1956-1959 . . . . . . . . . . . Mary Hester Instructor,
School of Nursing, Ogbomosho

1960-1962 . . . . . . . . . . . . Mary Hester Instructor,
                          School of Nursing, Eku
March 26, 1974 . . . . . . . . . . . . . . Carlyle passes
June 13, 1982 . . . . . . . . . . . . . . . . . Rosa passes

## Annotated List of Resources

### Books

Abodunde, Ayodeji. *A Heritage of Faith: A History of Christianity in Nigeria.* Pierce Watershed, 2017.

An exhaustive treatment of Nigerian Christian history but with merely paragraphs on Southern Baptist work there and no mention at all of the Powells. 804 pages.

Cauthen, Baker J. *Advance: A History Of Southern Baptist Foreign Missions.* Nashville: Broadman, 1970.

Estep, William R. *Whole Gospel Whole World: The Foreign Mission Board of the Southern Baptist Convention 1845-1995.* Nashville: Broadman & Holman, 1994.

High, Thomas O'Connor. *Outlined Notes on the Expansion of Baptist Work in Nigeria 1850-1939.* Ogbomoso: Nigerian Baptist Theological Seminary, 1970.

The seminary was kind enough to send me this short work by email attachment.

Hocutt, Hilliard Manly. *Struggling Upward.* author, 1951.

Long out of print, this book by one of Rosa Powell's brothers describes in detail the challenges of the Jefferson Davis Hocutt family. H. M. Hocutt was himself an early Associational Missionary who served the Buncombe (NC) Baptist Assocation. At this writing the book is available for reading from the East Carolina University digital library.

Holly, Howard. *Brief History of Burgaw Baptist Church: 1884-1974.*
A church history written by the church historian and published only to members and friends through duplicated copies.

James, Martha Elizabeth McArthur. *A Mixed Up Family: A Sampson County Autobiography 1852-1868.* Clinton NC: Taft Bass, 1955.
James was a step-sister of J. A. Powell (Carlyle's father). She offered her account of the Civil War period and its impact on the family of Luke Powell, whom her mother had married. Mrs. James (1847-1927) was in her early 70s when she wrote the account in pencil on a school copy book. Some of the anecdotes she recounted were included in Kathleen Snyder's *What Will They Do* Next. 35 pages.

Lambdin, Ina Smith. *Then Came Spring and Other Missionary Love Stories.* Author, 1969.
Rosa and Carlyle's story is chapter one of the book and the source of the title of the book. Lambdin indicated in the book she

gathered information on their story from them. There are ten missionary couples covered by a chapter each. 73 pages.

Oiness, Sylvia M. *Strange Fate of the Zamzam: The Miracle Ship.* Minneapolis: Nathaniel Carlson, 1942.
Account of a survivor - a missionary nurse. 38 page booklet. Pictures.

Powell, J. C. *112 Questions and Answers on Deaconship in Baptist Churches As Touching Problems in Nigeria.*
Published by Powell himself. These were actual questions natives had asked him during his work. Collected in 1935. Written in English and Yoruba. 19 page booklet.

Powell, J. C. *One Gross of Thoughts About the Master: Twelve in a Package.*
As the title suggests, 144 sentence statements about Christ arranged in 12 collections. Written in English. 14 page booklet.

Powell, J. C. and David Gasperson. *Impressions of Nigeria.* Gasperson, 2018.
Composed by J. C. Powell in the 1920s and modified slightly through the years, the manuscript was discovered in the possession of Mary Hester Powell and rewritten by David Gasperson. Published 2018 in advance of this biography.

Sadler, George W. *A Century in Nigeria*; Broadman. 1950.

A colleague of the Powells in Nigeria and then part of the support staff in Richmond, Sadler's book covers the period from 1850 to 1950 but with very little reference to the Powells. 151 pages.

Snyder, Kathleen Powell and Mamie Chambers Sawyer. *Our Kin*. Printed by authors, 1982.

Exhaustive genealogical records for the Powell, Bourden, Chamber and allied families of Eastern North Carolina. Photographs of family members, homes, churches, headstones and even furniture pieces. Never commercially published. Made available originally only to family and interested persons. 510 pages.

Snyder, Kathleen Powell and Mamie Chambers Sawyer. *What Will They Do Next*. Printed by authors, 1978.

Anecdotes of J. A. Powell, Mary Emma Bourden, their parents, his grandparents, and each of their 12 children. Pages 91-96 cover Carlyle, Rosa and Mary Hester. Photographs of family members. Never commercially published. Made available originally only to family and interested persons. 142 pages.

Swanson, S. Hjalmar, ed. *Zamzam: The Story of a Strange Missionary Odyssey*. Minneapolis: The Board of Foreign Missions of the Augustana Synod, 1941.

Coverage of the sinking of the *Zamzam* with many first-hand accounts by survivors, mostly from among the missionaries. Pictures. 149 pages.

## Collections

International Mission Board of the Southern Baptist Convention (formerly Foreign Mission Board)

Service files for Carlyle and Rosa have long been public information since their deaths. I requested and they granted release of Mary Hester's file. They were kind enough to send me digital downloads of those files, most of which consists of letters exchanged by the missionaries and their contacts at the Foreign Mission Board.

Mary Hester Powell correspondence, photos, manuscripts and memorabilia.

I was granted full access to extensive materials Mary Hester had kept over the years and the privilege to borrow those items for weeks as I needed them through the research and writing of the book.

Powell History Room, Warsaw (NC) Baptist Church

Mementoes, degrees, books from J. C.'s and Rosa's personal libraries, clothing items, furniture pieces, photos, yearbooks, and more.

Powell House resources

Multiple boxes of Kathleen Snyder's genealogical research, family anecdotes, photographs, copies of her books and those of others, and even a couple of furniture pieces from Nigeria acquired when we purchased the house at 603 N. Pine Street, Warsaw, NC.

*Tid Bits*

18 single-spaced, typed pages of Carlyle's recollections from his boyhood discovered in the material removed from the Powell House. I would learn he had written some of that material in letters to Mary Hester in 1939 and apparently collected it together and added to it. Mary Hester was pleased to get a copy of it. She'd not seen the collection before.

21690235R00146

Made in the USA
Middletown, DE
13 December 2018